40 DAYS
IN GOD'S BLESSING

40 DAYS

IN GOD'S BLESSING

A Devotional Encounter

REBECCA BARLOW JORDAN

WARNER
Faith®

New York Boston Nashville

Unless otherwise noted, Scripture quotations are taken from the HOLY BIBLE, NEW INTERNATIONAL VERSION®. NIV®. Copyright © 1973, 1978, 1984 by International Bible Society. Used by permission of Zondervan. All rights reserved.

Scriptures marked MSG are taken from The Message. Copyright © 1993, 1994, 1995, 1996, 2000, 2001, 2002. Used by permission of NavPress Publishing Group.

Scriptures noted NRSV are taken from the NEW REVISED STANDARD VERSION of the Bible. Copyright © 1989 by the Division of Christian Education of the National Council of the Churches of Christ in the USA. All rights reserved.

Scriptures noted NLT are taken from the *Holy Bible,* New Living Translation, copyright © 1996. Used by permission of Tyndale House Publishers, Inc., Wheaton, Illinois 60189. All rights reserved.

Scriptures noted KJV are taken from the King James Version of the Bible.

Scriptures noted TLB are taken from *The Living Bible,* copyright © 1971. Used by permission of Tyndale House Publishers, Inc., Wheaton, Illinois 60189. All rights reserved.

Warner Faith

1271 Avenue of the Americas, New York, NY 10020

Warner Faith® and the Warner Faith logo are registered trademarks.

Printed in the United States of America

First Edition: July 2006
10 9 8 7 6 5 4 3 2 1

The Library of Congress Cataloging-in-Publication Data

Jordan, Rebecca.
    40 days in God's blessing : a devotional encounter / Rebecca Barlow Jordan.—
1st ed.
        p. cm.
    ISBN-13: 978-0-446-57787-8
    ISBN-10: 0-446-57787-1
    1. Bible—Devotional use. 2. Christian life—Biblical teaching. 3. Devotional calendars. I. Title: Forty days in God's blessing. II. Title.
    BS617.8.J67 2006
    242'.2—dc22   2005035358

Book design by rlf design

To the Blessing Giver himself,

who alone deserves all honor, glory, and praise

CONTENTS

SPECIAL THANKS

It's impossible to write a book about God's blessing without thanking the special people behind the scenes who have been so helpful to me. I distinctly remember the day my cell phone rang and my agent, Steve Laube, cheerfully told me that Warner Faith wanted to publish my books. After my squeal of delight—which turned every head in the department store where I was shopping—my words to Steve were, "I feel so small." That feeling has only grown stronger. It always does, if you attempt to write about such a powerful subject as the intimacy of God, his character, his blessings—or anything about him. I not only feel small in the presence of such an awesome God, but I also feel humbled and deeply grateful for the privilege of working with a great company like Warner Faith.

I owe my editor, Leslie Peterson, many thanks for her encouragement, for working patiently with me, and for believing in my writing and in me. Thanks also to Holly Halverson for her thoroughness, patience and great editing skills in polishing this manuscript. To Rolf Zettersten, publisher of Warner Faith: thanks for believing in this project to its completion. I appreciate Jennette Munger, Cara Highsmith, Jana Burson, and so many others who played a part in finalizing this book. You are indeed a great blessing to me.

To Steve Laube, a great agent who has been a coach, encourager, instructor, and friend, thank you! These books would never have made it without your vision, belief, and placement. I appreciate your expertise and your belief in my writing!

So many have prayed this book through to completion and have offered encouragement throughout the process: my daughters and sons-in-law, Valerie, Jennifer, Shawn, and Craig, other family members, friends, members of the Bible study class I teach, fellow church members, and as always, my five faithful prayer warriors: Mary Griffin, Priscilla Adams, Sharon Hogan, Kim Coffman, and Ruth Inman.

There were days when I knew all these people made the difference: I felt their prayers in indescribable ways and could not have finished without them.

That was especially true with my husband's prayers and support. No one gives more encouragement than this man with whom I have shared life for thirty-nine years. He offered more than words, hugs, and editing suggestions. Larry gave me loving time, often taking over some of my work to free me for writing. He did whatever was necessary to help me complete this book and influenced this writing more than anyone else, so that together, we could be a team in ministry. Larry, thank you for your unselfish love and devotion. I love you and owe you so much! You are without a doubt one of God's greatest blessings to me!

And to the Blessing Giver himself, how can I thank God enough? He continues to pursue me, love me, teach me, and bless me in ways I could never deserve. To the Lord Jesus Christ, my best Friend, my Savior, the Lover of my soul: all my gratitude, love, and devotion. Lord, you are the one who makes me hunger and thirst for more of you, and you are the only one who can satisfy that desire. Thank you, Lord, for allowing me the privilege of writing about you and for you!

INTRODUCTION

Most authors follow the advice they receive early on: write what you know. That's what I have always tried to do. But the more you write about God and his character, the more you see you have barely scratched the surface. That's what happened when I wrote the first book in this devotional series—*40 Days in God's Presence*—as well as this book. It is my prayer that this book will further lead you to that same hunger and thirst for God himself.

When writing about God's blessing, it is a temptation to simply list all the good, tangible things God has ever done—or wants to do—and all the reasons why we should be grateful for those blessings. It didn't take me long in my study for this project, however, to realize that there are not enough books to contain all the blessings God has designed for those who know him. Psalm 40:5 says,

> *Many, O LORD my God,*
> *   are the wonders you have done.*
> *The things you planned for us*
> *   no one can recount to you;*
> *were I to speak and tell of them,*
> *   they would be too many to declare.*

I discovered some blessings quite unexpectedly. I hope these will challenge you to realize that not every gift is easily recognizable. Some may even appear as hindrances rather than blessings until you look farther and see God's heart. Nevertheless, I have chosen only a few—forty, to be exact.

I have not taken the route that says we deserve every good thing that comes to us. We deserve nothing. But the joy of knowing that God still wants to bless us and to give lavishly to us, when we are so undeserving, is almost impossible for me to understand at times.

God does love to bless his people. It is his nature to do so. He blessed Adam with a companion and gave them both a luxurious paradise in which to live and fellowship perfectly with their Creator. When sin separated us from him, God insisted on pouring out his greatest blessing: the gift of his own precious Son as Savior of the world. Relentlessly, he pursues us, loves us, and waits for us, so he can bless us even more in a hundred thousand ways.

Look at Jesus' last act as he ascended to his Father in heaven: "When he had led them out to the vicinity of Bethany, he lifted up his hands and blessed them. While he was blessing them, he left them and was taken up into heaven" (Luke 24:50-51). And soon after Jesus left, God sent the promised Holy Spirit—to bless his people with his daily presence.

God's blessings are as unique as the people he created. And while he may not work in your life in exactly the same way as he has in the lives of those in this book, you will find the principles are the same. If you spend even one day in God's blessing, I think you'll be amazed. But when you experience forty days with him, I hope you'll be changed forever. His adventures will thrill you; his grace will overwhelm you; his love will surprise you.

As you read this book, walk in the shadow of those gone before you and trace the footprints of God's faithfulness. But be prepared. Open your hands, your eyes, your ears, and your heart. I pray you'll be blessed as never before, and that you'll stand in God's presence, as I did, with overwhelming gratitude. And just when you think you've reached the end of his blessing, I hope you'll discover God has only just begun.

To write about my Father God is one of the greatest and most humbling honors he has ever given to me. I am not a scholar. This book is not a theological work, but a devotional encounter—at best, a challenge and invitation to you to experience him for yourself. Discover this God who loves you so completely and so unconditionally, and who wants to bless you every day of your life. In this book, may you find all the reasons you need to fall at his feet in a spirit of love, worship, and praise, crying out in grateful response, "God, how can *I* bless *you*?"

—*Rebecca*

40 DAYS

IN GOD'S BLESSING

HE CALLED US FRIENDS

"Abraham believed God,
and it was credited to him as righteousness,"
and he was called God's friend.

—James 2:23

She waited by the bedside of her lover of thirty-four years. Tenderly massaging his puffy hands, she studied his face, every line and wrinkle, as the tubes pumped life into her beloved. She watched the slow rise and fall of his chest and glanced periodically at the beeping, zigzag readings of the monitors above his bed. A smile glowed on her face even as a tear trickled down her cheek.

Priscilla loved her husband. Together they were the epitome of an intimate friendship. The two demonstrated what a devoted marriage could and should be like.

But intimacy always costs something: time, selflessness, thoughtfulness, trust—absolute trust. And very often, suffering. Those who are intimately close feel the hurts and joys of the ones they love more than anyone else.

As I watched Priscilla, I knew the blessing of this couple's intimacy was about to include something more: the ultimate suffering and sacrifice. As Thurman slipped away into the arms of his most intimate Friend, the Lord Jesus Christ, he left behind a legacy and example of true intimacy with his beloved wife.

Intimacy brings many pictures to mind. A man named Job though intimacy was something God demonstrated only by pouring out tangible blessings: good health, wealth, family, and friends. God often does that. In the middle of his suffering, Job said,

> Oh, for the day when I was in my prime,
> when God's intimate friendship blessed my house,
> when the Almighty was still with me
> and my children were around me,
> when my path was drenched with cream
> and the rock poured out for me streams of olive oil. (Job 29:4–6)

But intimate friendship includes more than warm blessings of love and prosperity. One of the ways God demonstrated its meaning was by choosing Abraham, a lone wanderer, to become his close friend.

We are not told how much Abraham (then known as Abram) knew about God when God first called him. Abraham grew up in the land of Ur, a city known as a center of pagan idolatry.[1] But God knew Abraham's heart when God said, "Leave your country . . . and go to the land I will show you" (Gen. 12:1). Intimacy with God meant Abraham had to abandon any preconceived ideas of success and follow this God he hardly knew to an unknown destination.

Intimacy always costs something.

So God made a covenant with Abraham and promised the following things: to make Abraham a great nation, to bless him, to make Abraham's name great, to make Abraham a blessing, to bless those who blessed Abraham, to curse those who cursed Abraham, and to bless all people on the earth through Abraham's son (Gen. 12:2–3, 21:12).

Fantastic promises! But what Abraham discovered was that the blessing of intimacy—the privilege of being God's friend—would cost something more. Abraham's journey took him through several tests of friendship, which Abraham failed a few times. Still, he hung with God, and God kept loving and leading him.

Years later, Abraham was a childless old man at ninety-nine. God was ready to make good on his promises. Still, more tests lay ahead. Did Abraham believe God would truly give him a son? In other words, did Abraham's friendship stand the test of faith? It did, and because Abraham believed, God "credited it to him as righteousness."

But the ultimate test of their intimate friendship came after the birth of Abraham's son, Isaac. This time, God required more than just belief. He asked for a demonstration of action—and ultimate surrender. What God asked Abraham to do—sacrifice his own son—God demanded from no one else in Scripture . . . but himself. Yet Abraham followed God, even when it looked as if it would cost his son—the answer to all of God's promises to Abraham.

What went through Abraham's mind early that morning as he cut the wood and saddled his donkey, preparing to travel to Moriah to make the sacrifice? How would God make Abraham a great nation if he killed his own son? How could God ask Abraham to slaughter his own flesh and blood—the miracle, the promised child he had finally borne? What did his two servants think as they set out along the dusty road to Mount Moriah? Did Abraham ever question, "What are you thinking, God?"

> What God asked Abraham to do—sacrifice his own son—God demanded from no one else in Scripture . . . but himself.

And what about Isaac? Did he get a little nervous when Abraham tied his hands and laid him on the altar with the wood? When Abraham raised a knife to plunge into Isaac's chest, did he cry out, "Father, what are you thinking?" (Gen. 22:1-10).

The question is not what God or anyone else was *thinking*, but what Abraham *believed*. Looking back, the New Testament clues us in to Abraham's thinking *and* beliefs:

> *By faith Abraham, when God tested him, offered Isaac as a sacrifice. He who had received the promises was about to sacrifice his one and only son, even though God had said to him, "It is through Isaac that your offspring will be reckoned." Abraham reasoned that God could raise the dead, and figuratively speaking, he did receive Isaac back from death. (Hebrews 11:17–19)*

Abraham obeyed and passed the test proving his genuine faith, friendship, and trust in God. Just before Abraham was about to plunge the knife into Isaac's body, God stopped him and provided a substitute lamb for a burnt offering.

In the provision of that lamb, we see a foreshadowing of God's own Son, laid on the sacrificial altar of a cross, crucified for you and me. Why? Because God wanted a love relationship with us. Because intimacy costs something: it cost God his own Son. Yet when Jesus died, God proved his intention to make us all his intimate friends. Jesus said to his disciples before he died, "I have called you friends" (John 15:15). His words included us as well.

What does true intimacy cost us? A lifelong commitment to the one who pursues us and loves us and calls us his own. True intimacy comes from an obedient trust: "I believe." The result is a deep oneness with God. God counted Abraham's faith as the basis for his intimate friendship, and it's where the blessing of intimacy with God always begins.

Like Abraham, may it be said of us: "That one is a friend of God!"

PERSONAL TRUTH

True intimacy means a death to our own selfish desires.

PERSONAL PRAYER

Lord, thank you for making me your intimate friend through your death on the cross. When tests come my way, help me to follow you no matter what happens. May the joy of our friendship radiate to others so that they, too, want to become your friends.

PERSONAL QUESTION

How has God's intimate friendship blessed you?

THE GRACE PLACE

"Then neither do I condemn you," Jesus declared.
"Go now and leave your life of sin."

—John 8:11

No one seemed to notice as a woman entered the sanctuary late. Hearty songs of praise filled the large auditorium, but the woman's heart felt heavy. She looked around at the well-dressed crowd. Her eyes caught the glance of an older deacon, and for a moment, he stared.

Maybe she should leave. Just as the woman turned to go, an older couple hemmed her in on one side. She turned to the left, and a family of five scooted in to sandwich her. *Trapped.* Why had she come, anyway? She didn't belong there. Her life was in shambles. She knew no one. And no one cared to know her—she was sure of that. She had only wanted to find a little peace, a little . . . something she couldn't explain.

The music stopped, and the preacher began to speak. To leave now would cause a stir and call attention to herself. She had never felt so alone. . . .

She wasn't alone. Another woman had felt the same way. She would have given anything to leave, but some angry men had driven her to this place and had shoved her to the ground in front of Jesus. Everywhere she looked, she was hemmed in by jeering people. She didn't belong there in the temple court, and she felt totally worthless as she endured the stares of onlookers where Jesus was teaching.

The Pharisees, those teachers of the Law, had probably been plotting all week, watching her every move. They knew when the woman crept out after dark, and when she returned home before dawn. They had spies in secret places.

> Jesus stooped to the ground, then quietly, methodically, began writing something in the dirt with his finger.

It was the only life she knew. Caught in a spiral of sin, she had searched for love in all the wrong places. But that day was the right time, wrong place for the Pharisees. They finally caught her in the very act of adultery and had dragged her to Jesus like a bag of trash. They were not trying to teach the woman a lesson, nor were they seeking to clean up the streets by prosecuting prostitutes. Those law-keepers cared about only one thing: to catch Jesus in a trap.

As always, they wanted not to shame the woman but to discredit Jesus—to put him out of business. Jesus represented the greatest threat to their rigid ritual-keeping.

The Mosaic Law called for stoning a woman caught in adultery. Now, wouldn't Jesus agree? Would *he* defy God's own law? The crowd began to chime in with the Pharisees' accusations. What would Jesus do?

Filled with shame, the woman didn't dare to look up. She covered her head and her ears, as if to shut out the taunts and protect herself from the flying stones. She was too young to die. But according to Moses' Law, she knew her behavior warranted it.

Jesus stooped to the ground, then quietly, methodically, began writing something in the dust with his finger. The Pharisees continued to throw other questions his way, so Jesus hurled a "stone" of his own with these words: "If any one of you is without sin, let him be the first to throw a stone at her" (John 8:7). Then Jesus stooped to the ground again and resumed his doodling in the sand.

Those legalists didn't understand, as Max Lucado says, "judging others is the quick and easy way to feel good about ourselves." None of us has the right to judge. Lucado adds, "Can the hungry accuse the beggar? Can the sick mock the ill? Can the blind judge the deaf? Can the sinner condemn the sinner? No. Only One can judge."[2] That one was hunched on the ground in front of them, writing something.

Slowly the people left, until only two remained: the accused woman and Jesus. He spoke with a tender but authoritative voice to her. "Woman, where are they? Has no one condemned you?"

The woman raised her head and looked around cautiously. Her eyes met Jesus' and she replied with genuine respect, "No one, sir."

"Then neither do I condemn you." Jesus' words did not condone her sin. But with these six words, he freed the woman's spirit and allowed her to leave a changed woman. To be pardoned only to reenter a life of sinfulness would profit her nothing. But when Jesus himself spoke those pointed words to her, "Go now and leave your life of sin," she knew nothing would ever be the same (John 8:1–11). . . .

The sermon ended. The invitation began, and the woman's heart beat wildly. *What will they think? Will they condemn me? Will they point fingers?* She looked around, realizing she had no place to hide. Panic struck. Just about the time she decided to bolt past the couple, the older woman moved closer, took the young woman's

> Grace allows you to abandon your hiding place forever.

hand in hers, and whispered something in her ear. Taken by surprise, the younger woman began to cry softly and nod her head. Together they walked to the altar and knelt.

When the young woman stood up and turned around, the pastor was smiling, and people had formed a line to come by and hug her. No one pointed a finger at her. No one condemned her. She left that day a changed woman, eager to abandon her old life and begin a new one.

And what did the older woman whisper to her earlier? It was the same word Jesus might have written on the ground beside the condemned woman: *grace*.

We can't earn it. We can't buy it. Grace is a gift—pure and free. Jesus already purchased it with his life (Eph. 2:8–9). "But is it enough?" you ask. Does God's grace really cover everything? Some of us still hang out in what we think are our safe hiding places, saying such things as: "God can't accept me." "I'm not good enough." "You don't know what I did." "What if I mess up again?" God's grace is sufficient, and it is complete (2 Cor. 12:9).

Grace does not grant us a license to repeat our sinful habits, just so God can give us more grace (Rom. 6:1). Jesus said, "Go . . . and leave your life of sin." Grace changes our hearts: it motivates our actions, it renews our minds, it frees our souls. Without grace, failure has no value. Without grace, service has no benefit. Without grace, there is no gift. And without the gift, there is no Giver. Grace allows you to abandon your hiding place forever.

The only one who can drag us into God's "temple court" is our enemy, Satan. But when he does, Jesus simply stoops and writes something on the floor of heaven: *grace*. Satan, on the other hand, has no words left. Lucado says, "Grace means you don't have to run anymore! It's the truth. Grace means it's finally safe to turn yourselves in."[3]

Grace is a blessing—undeserved and incomparable. And when Jesus writes it on our hearts or whispers it in our ears, there is only one logical response: receive it and enjoy it.

There's no other blessing like it.

PERSONAL TRUTH

Grace is the place you can visit anytime you want.

PERSONAL PRAYER

Father, I can never repay you for the grace you have given to me. I don't understand it, and I'll never deserve it, but like a child with a gift at Christmas, I gladly receive it. You and your grace are amazing.

PERSONAL QUESTION

How has God's grace changed you?

HAIR TODAY, GONE TOMORROW

O Sovereign LORD, remember me.
O God, please strengthen me just once more.

—Judges 16:28

Someone once said, "Greatness lies not in being strong, but in the right use of strength." What a shame that a man named Samson didn't learn that early in his life.

God's chosen people, the Israelites, had begun an endless cycle of rebellion. And their dreaded enemy, the Philistines (remember the giant Goliath?), had enslaved them for forty years. The people cried out to God, and he sent them a champion of deliverance. Then the cycle repeated again (Judg. 13:1). During the years following Samson's death, things grew even worse. The Bible records in Israel's "state of ungodly union" address, "In those days Israel had no king; everyone did what he saw fit" (Judg. 17:6).

Apparently Samson did "what he saw fit" as well. Born to godly parents, Samson had been sanctified by God even before his birth. An angel of the Lord, later identified as the Lord himself, appeared to Manoah and his barren wife and announced they would bear a child. He gave precise instructions on how to raise their son: as a Nazarite. A Nazarite was a person voluntarily set apart to God for a certain period of time (see Num. 6). But in this case, the Lord told the parents it was God's intention for the boy, Samson, to keep these vows for a lifetime. Among the vows were not drinking wine, not touching anything dead, and not shaving his head (Judg. 13:2–7).

Things went fine until Samson grew to young adulthood. Then he acted out his own desires, breaking almost every facet of the Nazarite vows. Samson had a secret source of strength known only to his parents and himself. But perhaps not even they understood the real reason for his miraculous might.

> The secret lay in his relationship with God—and in his obedience.

Samson started out by marrying a foreigner—a Philistine woman—to which his parents objected. He ate honey from a beehive in the dead carcass of a lion, defiling himself and breaking part of his vow. Through trickery, Samson lost his wife to another man before Samson could consummate the marriage. So Samson used his unusual strength to get revenge and massacre thirty men. Later he burned the Philistines' fields, and in return they burned the woman and her father to death.

Samson eventually found another love, a beautiful and enticing woman named Delilah. But Delilah seemed more interested in saving face than in saving her lover's life. The Philistines tried to get to Samson by offering Delilah silver if she uncovered the source of Samson's strength. She nagged Samson repeatedly, but each time, Samson tricked her and used his strength to break free. Finally in a weak moment, Samson gave in, tired of the incessant nagging: "The secret of my strength is in my hair. If they cut my hair, I will no longer be strong" (see Judg. 16:17).

What Samson didn't know was that the secret to his strength really had nothing to do with his hair. The secret lay in his relationship with God—and in his obedience. God kept his part of the covenant. But when Samson broke the last stipulation of the vow by revealing his secret and allowing someone to cut his hair, God removed his power from Samson's life.

Finally captured and maimed by the Philistines, Samson was blind, weak, and reduced to a circus spectacle. He was a broken man. For most of his selfish life, revenge had consumed him, and he had used his supernatural strength to get what he wanted, when he wanted it. He would have done well to learn from someone who realized what true strength can do to make a difference. Sometimes it takes the "weak" to motivate us to use our strength in unselfish ways.

That's what happened to Keller Christensen. A hefty linebacker and special team player for Oregon State, Keller netted numerous tackles and a touchdown against Arizona State when he recovered a fumble on a punt return. At 209 pounds, Keller was sturdily built. He and Samson had at least a couple of things in common: physical strength—and long hair. Both lost their long locks to a pair of scissors—but Keller "lost" his intentionally.

Samson's hair had never been cut since birth. Keller had grown his hair for two and a half years. But when this football player learned about Locks of Love, an organization that provides young and financially challenged cancer patients with wigs, he turned into a man on a mission. He used an inner strength and joined thousands of others who have donated their long hair (he gave sixteen inches) to Locks of Love. Keller's and many others' contributions to those who are weak, sick, and less fortunate bring a new sense of hope and strength to kids under eighteen.[4]

> Sometimes it takes the "weak" to motivate us to use our strength in unselfish ways.

Some begin strong and end weak. Samson, repentant and desirous to make a difference with his death even if he had squandered his life, begged God for one last chance to use his strength rightly. God heard Samson's humble cry. During a festive Philistine celebration and sacrifice to their god, the Philistines brought Samson out to boast his capture and to taunt him. Samson, now blind but determined, asked a servant to lead him to the pillars of the great temple. With both hands pressed against the massive pillars supporting the temple, Samson pushed with all of his strength. The temple came crashing down. Scores of people—including three thousand men and women watching from the roof, and Samson—died that day. The Bible says, "Thus he killed many more when he died than while he lived" (Judg. 16:30).

Thousands of years later, Samson is listed among the great faith warriors of the Bible (Heb. 11:32). In the end, God turned Samson's weakness to strength and destroyed some of Israel's greatest enemies.

The real secret of our strength is this: the one who understands he is totally weak apart from God will stand head and shoulders above any giant of a man. With God's help, the psalmist David said even the weak can "advance against a troop; / . . . [or] scale a wall." David added, "It is God who arms me with strength" (Ps. 18:29, 32).

God does not bless us with strength to use it selfishly, just to attain our own desires or to feed a vengeful spirit. Those who know the true secret—and Source—of their strength indeed know how to use and enjoy this gift rightly: to bless others, and to bless God himself.

PERSONAL TRUTH

Strength becomes new with the power of two.

PERSONAL PRAYER

Lord, when I am weak, you are strong. Thank you for blessing me with your Spirit's presence, for you will always be the secret—and the true Source—of my strength.

PERSONAL QUESTION

In what areas do you most need God's strength?

FROM THE MOUTHS OF BABES

I tell you the truth,
anyone who will not receive the kingdom of God like a little child
will never enter it.

—Mark 10:15

The house is quiet again. No more screams of delight, no more tiny fingers wrapped around mine, no more bubbles in my hair or laughter in the air. No more sticky kisses and tight hugs. No more, "Look, Mimi! Look, Papa!" The grandchildren have gone home.

It's no wonder God loves children. Wide-eyed and innocent, hearts still tender, virgin minds yet untainted by pride or skepticism, these little ones touch the heartstrings of their Creator. Children trust deeply, love fully, and see life simply. They may question, but they readily accept authoritative answers and are always eager to please the ones they love.

Some treat children more as useless objects than as precious gifts. But a look through the pages of Scripture reveals the importance of children and the position they hold in God's eyes. If you look carefully, you might find these headlines:

Child Promised by God Born to Aging Parents [Genesis 21:1–5]
Egyptian Princess Rescues Infant from Crocodile-Infested
   Waters [Exodus 2:1–10]

Child Raised from the Dead [1 Kings 17:19–22]
Girl Instrumental in Army Commander's Healing
   [2 Kings 5:1–14]
Eight-Year-Old King Turns People Back to God [2 Kings 23:1–3]
Son of God Comes to Earth as a Baby [Luke 2:8–15]
Boy's Lunch Feeds Thousands [John 6:8–13]
Jesus Heals Demonic Boy [Luke 9:37–43]

The Old Testament law indicated that children were a sign of God's blessing (Deut. 28:4). The psalmist said children are God's gift to us; they are our rewards (Ps. 127:3). God has taught children how to praise him with pure hearts that shame their enemies—and sometimes us as well (Ps. 8:2). How many times my own children reminded me of Bible truths hidden in their little hearts—principles I needed to hear but had temporarily misplaced during times of stress or difficulty.

So strong were Jesus' emotions about children that he rebuked the disciples when they tried to prevent pint-sized admirers from climbing into his lap. Eager voices, laughing hearts, chubby fingers reached out for him. How beautiful their voices! What honesty and love they offered! How they touched Jesus' heart, even as he laid his hands on them with heaven's blessing. Jesus knew only those with childlike hearts of faith could understand—and experience—heaven's joyful blessings.

> Jesus knew only those with childlike hearts of faith could understand—and experience—heaven's joyful blessings.

Even the chief priests and teachers who observed Jesus' miracles failed to understand the children's praise-filled exclamations: "When the religious leaders saw the outrageous things he was doing, and heard all the children running and shouting through the Temple, 'Hosanna to David's Son!' they were up in arms and took him to task. 'Do you hear what these children are saying?'" Jesus even commended them: "Yes, I hear them. And haven't you read in God's Word, 'From the mouths of children and babies I'll furnish a place of praise?'" (Matt. 21:15-16 MSG).

Jesus used a little child to teach his disciples on more than one occasion. The disciples were arguing one day about which of them might become heaven's most important saint. Jesus read their thoughts and stood a young one beside him to show the difference between childish attitudes and childlike faith. "Whoever accepts this child as if the child were me, accepts me," he said. "And whoever accepts me, accepts the One who sent me. You become great by accepting, not asserting. Your spirit, not your size, makes the difference" (Luke 9:48 MSG). At that moment, I imagine the disciples felt very . . . small.

You may never see Roy Hutchinson's name in the Hall of Fame. But Roy knew about accepting children. And it wasn't his size—he stood six-foot-two—that made the difference, but his gentle spirit. He was working as a paramedic in 1984 when Tiffany was born to a mentally challenged mother, who hadn't realized she was pregnant. He heard about the baby in critical condition and went to see her. The umbilical cord had been wrapped around her neck and shut off her brain's oxygen. Tiffany had brain damage, cerebral palsy, and was deformed in many ways. But Roy thought she was beautiful.

When he discovered Tiffany would probably die in an institution, he and his wife took her home and subsequently adopted her. During the next few years Roy and his wife divorced, and his own son was killed in a car accident. But for fifteen years Roy accepted and tenderly cared for Tiffany. Together they shared a bond that few would understand. Roy had biked all across the country, but he said Tiffany

> Children indeed teach us more about life, love, and family, and we are blessed by their presence.

was the teacher who had "taught him about life, love, and family." After Tiffany's death in 2000, Roy admitted, "I always wondered whether two parents couldn't have done it better. But then she'd smile, and I knew nobody could love her more than me."[5]

Children really are blessings. Whether we have a family of children by natural birth or adoption, or we simply surround ourselves with the happy laughter of neighborhood children, they cannot help but touch our lives. Can you imagine a world without them?

Children indeed teach us more about life, love, and family. But they also teach us about heaven. God wants to give us the heart and the eyes of a child. That childlike wonder and faith make us run to him as God's children again and again to be touched, loved, and blessed with his wonderful presence.

Hearts hardened by doubt, pride, and selfishness will find the keys to God's kingdom in the hands of a child. Someone has said, "The trouble with a child is that he can't grow up to be anything but an adult." But even as adults, when we humble ourselves like little children, needy and trusting and eager to please our Father's heart, he will unleash the secrets and blessings of his kingdom— and make us his true children indeed.

PERSONAL TRUTH

A child is a reflection of heaven's tenderness.

PERSONAL PRAYER

Father, thank you for the blessing of children. Make my heart like that of a child. Let me see your world through eyes filled with wonder and faith. And thank you for making me your own child.

PERSONAL QUESTION

Would God call your attitudes childish or childlike?

SURPRISE, SURPRISE, SURPRISE!

Surprise us with love at daybreak;
then we'll skip and dance all the day long.

—Psalm 90:14 MSG

I should be used to them by now. Life is full of them. But every now and then, God's little surprises catch me off guard.

A few years ago I was attending a conference and had just stepped off the plane. While I was waiting for my luggage, a large man approached me and spoke boldly: "If you're not already in ministry, you're going to be in ministry."

I stepped back with raised eyebrows, totally surprised. But he continued to speak. "The Lord is going to lay on you a blessing and an anointing and greatly use you for him."

I already felt that God had blessed me more than I could ever deserve. Surely the man had mistaken me for someone else. "I am a minister's wife . . . and . . . a writer," I stammered, feeling as though I needed to respond somehow. But the man ignored my words and continued his message. Finally I asked point-blank, "Why would you tell me this?"

He never paused. "Because God told me to." And the man walked away. I never saw him again. I asked my friends who had witnessed this scene to verify what the man had just told me.

I was shaken, but totally open. Under my breath I prayed, "God, if this is truly a word from you, would you please confirm and let me in on it?"

I enjoyed that little surprise from God until I stepped into the hotel moments later. For the next three days, I felt as if I had entered a war zone. Anxious and fearful thoughts fired rockets at me nonstop. At one point, near panic, I escaped to my room to desperately seek God's face—and the meaning for such confused emotions.

> Every now and then, God's little surprises catch me off guard.

Finally, on the third day, God began to speak peace to my weary mind, through the speakers, through the worship, through my time alone as I cried out to him. By the time Monday morning arrived, I felt refreshed and strangely renewed. But God's surprises continued.

Only two days before, I had avoided strangers. Now I sought them out and felt compelled to pray for them. I saw people not as possible networks but as God's children with needs. At a restaurant later I shared my testimony when someone in a nearby booth inquired about the religious subject of my conversation. Everywhere I turned I felt a strange sense of God's presence.

That same day, after a speakers' luncheon, a worship leader I greatly respect asked if she could talk with me. "God has given me a word for you," she said.

This time I simply smiled and listened. Her words, though different, confirmed the first message: "You are on the verge of going deeper with God. There are areas of darkness in your life, and God wants to give you total freedom to minister for him. He wants to bless you greatly." I knew about those dark areas. I had experienced some only days earlier. She continued with a Scripture exhortation, and I agreed to read the passages she recommended. I longed to be free of any lingering fears.

Still pondering the weekend's surprises, both good and bad, I asked my Father a bit timidly, "Um, God, would it be too much trouble for you to confirm your words one more time and let me know these are truly messages from your heart?" I love God's patience. In the next few months, he did so—several times, in different ways. Little by little, God is removing the fears and other areas of darkness and replacing them with new freedom, boldness, and passion—and a continual hunger for more of him. Whatever he does, or doesn't do with my life in the future is entirely up to him. I'm content to keep trusting him and enjoying whatever surprises he brings my way.

Someone else experienced one of God's surprises and his subsequent confirmation. The Lord surprised and commended a God-fearing man named Cornelius through an angel, then instructed him to send for Peter to deliver the rest of the surprise. Now Cornelius was a Gentile, and typically Jews like Peter did not associate with those outside their faith. Still, Cornelius sent his servants to bring Peter to his home.

About the same time that Cornelius's servants entered Peter's gate, Peter was praying on the rooftop of his house, pondering the surprise vision God had just given him: a large sheet filled with all kinds of animals, both clean and unclean according to Jewish Law. God had told Peter, "Kill and eat." At first Peter protested that he never ate "unclean" foods, but God told him not to "call anything impure that God has made clean" (Acts 10:13, 15).

> Some of God's surprises leave us with a sense of wonder.

When the Spirit instructed Peter to accompany Cornelius's servants to the man's home, Peter realized the meaning of the vision: that God does not show favoritism and accepts all who turn to him (Acts 10:34). This was the beginning of the gospel's spreading to Gentiles. The Holy Spirit confirmed Peter's good news, and Cornelius's entire household was baptized (Acts 10).

At times God's surprises may not seem pleasant. In fact, they may seem distasteful and bothersome, like Elisha's instructions to Naaman to go dip in the muddy Jordan River seven times to cure his leprosy. This important army commander fully expected the prophet to deliver a word from God that was more suitable to a man of his importance. In fact, he envisioned Elisha as some sort of magician who would "call on the name of the LORD his God, wave his hand over the spot and cure me of my leprosy" (2 Kings 5:11). Yet when Naaman humbled himself and obeyed, God cured him on the seventh dip.

Some of God's surprises astonish us and leave us with a sense of wonder. But not all of God's surprises make sense at the time and may seem more like intrusions. James refers to those as "trials." But God is never caught off guard. He will use those trials to purify us, prune us, and grow us to completion. God's ultimate goal is to make us more like himself. James said we are to treat even those surprises as "sheer gift[s]" (James 1:2 MSG). *Blessings,* in other words.

Even though I'm still tempted to do it, I am discovering it is not always necessary to analyze the surprises God sends our way. To be sure, we must evaluate the accuracy of anyone's "word from the Lord"—which needs to line up with God's character and his written Word—and receive the counsel of wise, godly servants. But it's also important to trust that God has a plan and a path for us to follow, even when we don't understand how it will unfold. If we insist on looking at all of life through skeptical, theological sunglasses, we will miss some of God's best surprises. If we truly believe that God is deeply committed to us and has our best interests at heart, perhaps at times we simply need to respond like a child: "Thank you, God! I just love surprises!"

One thing we can count on: no matter how they appear at the time, God's surprises are always good.

PERSONAL TRUTH

When God speaks, we would be wise to listen.

PERSONAL PRAYER

More than comfort, more than blessing, more than anything, Lord, I want you. Burn your words in my heart, and make me useable for your service. Thank you for every surprise you send my way.

PERSONAL QUESTION

How long has it been since you recognized one of God's surprises?

BREATHING LESSONS

Since they could not get him to Jesus because of the crowd,
they made an opening in the roof above Jesus and,
after digging through it,
lowered the mat the paralyzed man was lying on.

—Mark 2:4

In her book *The Creative Call*, Janice Elsheimer relates the story of how artist Mary Engelbreit found her way through a maze of discouragement to enjoy the blessing of God's creativity:

When Mary was nearing high-school graduation, she told her guidance counselor that she wanted to pursue the desire of her heart—to illustrate children's books. The counselor disdainfully told her, "You can't do that. You've got to be practical. Get a degree in English so you can teach." Ignoring that advice, Mary got a job at an art supply shop, learned all she could about different media and how to use them, and got to know all kinds of working artists. Once she realized that people actually did make a living as artists, she turned her energies and talents toward making her dream a reality. Mary Engelbreit overcame the discouraging words of others to become one of the world's most successful commercial artists.

Whenever she became disheartened, Engelbreit would remember how, even at a young age, her parents had encouraged her to pursue her artwork. When she was nine, Mary announced that she needed a

27

studio, and her mother promptly converted a linen closet into one for her. "From that time on," Engelbreit says, "my parents always treated my art as serious business. Bolstered by their support, I continued on even without formal training, telling myself over and over what they had instilled in me: 'Of course you can become an artist. Keep working on it. If you can imagine it, you can achieve it. If you can dream it, you can become it.'"[6]

> Because creativity is a gift from God, every artist and author understands the importance of listening to the Creator in order to find the direction and inspiration he or she needs.

Four men also faced a maze of discouragement. They were not artists, musicians, or poets. Yet they pooled their creative energies and overcame a myriad of obstacles—and the results were nothing short of genius.

The four men wanted to see Jesus, but they faced a major roadblock: Jesus' fame had followed him into Capernaum, where crowds of people gathered around the house in which he was teaching. Like senior citizens at a free buffet, the masses probably arrived early, cramming every nook and cranny, hoping to find a full meal of hope and encouragement from this Miracle Worker. But the small, thatch-roofed house could hold only so many. A line of people snaked into the street, each person shushing the others so he could hear Jesus' voice.

A paralytic man, carried by four men on a makeshift stretcher, was at the back of the line. Perhaps the four men mirrored the thoughts of others in the crowd: *If we can just get to Jesus, we can find healing!* They were not seeking anything for themselves, however, except perhaps the joy of seeing this man's hopes and dreams realized. We're not even told if the man himself expressed the desire to be there, or if these fellows suggested it. But we do know they were men who recognized an important truth: hindrances to Jesus *can* be overcome.

Author Madeleine L'Engle believes creativity requires "being time." Because creativity is a gift from God, every artist and author understands the importance of listening to the Creator in order to find the direction and inspiration he or she needs. Elsheimer alludes to this process as "breathing in." But she says completing the creative process requires "breathing out."[7] Others might call it "putting feet to our prayers and our faith."

The four friends did not stop at "breathing in" Jesus' words. They "breathed them out" and followed through, achieving what appeared to be an impossible dream to everyone else. Carefully they removed a portion of the mud-hardened roof and began to gently lower the paralytic to the floor. When the flying mud pieces and dust had settled, the man lay in front of Jesus.

Jesus did not see a hopeless case, an interruption, or an impossible task. The first thing the Bible says he saw was the men's faith! He recognized their creativity, then exercised some of his own. Instead of immediately telling the man to rise and be healed—which many expected—Jesus made a bold statement that riled the Creator's critics, the teachers of the Law standing nearby.

Looking directly at the paralytic, Jesus said, "Son, your sins are forgiven" (Mark 2:5). Jesus' critics called his words blasphemy. Healing was one thing, but in their minds, forgiving sins was another—and without question, a divine act. "Who does this Jesus think he is, God himself?"

> Many wannabes have tried and failed, simply because they stopped at "breathing in."

Jesus was indeed God—in the flesh. And he chose to heal the man both physically *and* spiritually. Why? Both required divine intervention. Jesus was not trying to honor the man or himself, but to prove he had the divine authority to do both: heal and forgive. His actions not only confirmed his divinity; they brought honor and glory to his Father—

Jesus' ultimate purpose in everything he did. When the people witnessed the man's complete healing, they praised God.

True creativity does not stop at the stage of inspiration. Many wannabes have tried and failed simply because they stopped at "breathing in." They failed to overcome the hindrances around them. But the true artist sees the completed picture by faith.

All of us are artists, in one way or another, and God has "breathed in" a work for us to do. And God certainly allows and encourages us to enjoy the fruits of our labor. But the true blessing comes not just in knowing that we have overcome. The joy wells up when our creativity validates its divine origin and ultimately brings honor and glory not to us or to the work itself, but to our Father God.

Personal Truth

His inspiration often brings us perspiration.

Personal Prayer

Lord, thank you for the inspiration of your Spirit that fills, corrects, teaches, and breathes life into everything you ask me to do. You are the Author of creativity itself. That you would allow me a part in that is a wonder and a privilege beyond words. May my work—and my life—always result in praise and glory to you.

Personal Question

Has God given you any "breathing lessons" lately?

IT'S ALL ABOUT HIM

The God of heaven will give us success.

—Nehemiah 2:20

Another touchdown, another goal reached for a team victory. Yet where was the team in all of this? A lone running back had pushed through the wall of defensive linemen trying to tackle him. Triumphantly, he lunged over the goal line for six points. Then suddenly, he broke into a well-rehearsed and carefully choreographed dance, beating his chest like a caged gorilla and communicating by his actions, "Look at me—I'm the man!" Clearly, it was all about him.

The ball changed hands and the opposing team ran the ball back on the ensuing kickoff eighty yards for a touchdown. The kick returner, in sharp contrast to his opponent, knelt for a moment as if in silent prayer, then quietly joined his teammates as they celebrated together the answering score. Same scenario, different results.

Another "player" emerged in biblical history centuries before the birth of Christ. Jewish by birth, he survived the Jewish exile and rose to the high position of the king's cupbearer in the Persian court. For over five hundred years, the Jewish people had lived as slaves under Persian rule, then were finally released. One hundred years later, the temple in Jerusalem had been rebuilt—but the people still lived outside the broken-down walls of Jerusalem.

Devoid of hope, leadership, and purpose, the former exiles simply blended in with a land filled with foreigners. Their heritage was slipping away under the dominion of some influential local politicians.[8]

Nehemiah knew how to get on praying ground with God. He didn't learn that in a day.

Enter Nehemiah. Why would he care? He lived a life of moderate luxury, of influence, of position. When one of his Jewish brothers brought him a report about Jerusalem's condition, the broken-down walls, and the people's broken-down spirits, why did Nehemiah suddenly decide to take action?

Because God had given Nehemiah the blessing of leadership. How do we recognize that blessing? By looking at Nehemiah's character. What was his immediate reaction? He had not experienced their hardships, yet he was so burdened for the people and the city where his fathers were buried that he denied himself palace luxuries and "sat down and wept. For some days I mourned and fasted and prayed before the God of heaven" (Neh. 1:4).

Nehemiah had not forgotten his roots—who he was. Most importantly, he had not forgotten who God was. His prayer didn't begin, "It's all about us." Instead, he immediately started addressing and acknowledging the characteristics of God. He reminded God of his faithfulness and God's covenant with his people (Neh. 1:5).

Nehemiah was persistent, praying not once, but many days. He agreed with God about his nation's sins, identifying himself and his family as ones who "have acted very wickedly toward you" (Neh. 1:7). Then Nehemiah once again reminded God of his promise to reassemble his exiled people—a covenant given to Moses long before. Nehemiah knew how to get on praying ground with God. He didn't learn that in a day.

Nehemiah finished his prayer by asking for success and appealed to God as one of his servants "who delight in revering your name" (Neh. 1:11).

Between the lines, Nehemiah was saying, "I know who you are, God, and I know who we are. We are your people. But we have turned away, and we are coming back to acknowledge you once more. It will be your hand, not ours, that gives us success. You are the only one who can."

Throughout the book of Nehemiah you can find God's blessing of leadership exemplified in Nehemiah's life. He knew how to make a godly appeal and had a godly plan of action (Neh. 2:3–9). He encouraged his fellow Israelites and showed them how to respond to the heckling of opposing politicians with God-confidence (Neh. 2:20).

He was an organizer and could delegate responsibility. And each time the Israelites met opposition, Nehemiah returned again to the secret of his success. He was a man of prayer who trusted completely in God (Neh. 4:9, 14, 20, 6:9). The blessing of leadership also included discernment; Nehemiah saw through the schemes of fellow prophets. And throughout their deceitful attempts, Nehemiah never faltered (Neh. 6:1–14).

When God's people finally finished the work, God topped off Nehemiah's success with the ultimate blessing: God received all the credit and all the glory. The Bible says when the enemy nations heard about the amazing reconstruction of the massive walls in only fifty-two

> When God wants to give the blessing of leadership, he knows what kind of man or woman to pursue.

days, they "lost their self-confidence, because they realized that this work had been done with the help of our God" (Neh. 6:16).

The remainder of the book of Nehemiah is filled with the fruits of Nehemiah's blessing. He was not the only one who enjoyed

God's goodness. In fact, God's reason for that blessing was not just for Nehemiah's sake. Someone once said, "The business of a leader is to turn weakness into strength, obstacles into stepping stones, and disaster into triumph." Nehemiah fit that description well. When God wants to give the blessing of leadership, he knows what kind of man or woman to pursue. And everyone that leader influences is the recipient of God's widespread, joyful blessing.

At the dedication of the newly rebuilt Jerusalem walls, the people "offered great sacrifices, rejoicing because God had given them great joy. . . . The sound of rejoicing in Jerusalem could be heard far away" (Neh. 12:43).

In a sense, everyone is a leader, because someone is always watching or following you. Remember, with the blessing of leadership comes a responsibility. The success and enjoyment of God's ultimate purpose may rest in your willingness to use that blessing well.

Truly, it really isn't about you. It's all about him.

PERSONAL TRUTH

A leader is someone who first learned how to follow.

PERSONAL PRAYER

Lord, help me to keep my eyes on you, so that those following close behind may see you clearly and discover your faithfulness and blessing, too.

PERSONAL QUESTION

Is God's blessing of leadership a joy—or a burden—to you?

LOSS OR GAIN?

But rejoice that you participate in the sufferings of Christ,
so that you may be overjoyed when his glory is revealed.

—1 Peter 4:13

Thousands of spectators had gathered for this momentous occasion in Rome. The crowds, thirsty for blood, began to shout. "More! More! More!" Nero, the half-crazed emperor who was trying to blame "Christ-ones" for the troubles of his empire, pointed to his victims waiting behind iron gates, as if to say, "Is this what you want?"

A huge cheer arose from the grand amphitheater. Nero motioned to another gate, where the fierce carnivores waited for their sport. The roar of the crowd overpowered the rumblings of the pacing beasts. "Yes! Yes! Yes! Yes!" cried the onlookers. "Let the show start!"

Slowly the first gate swung open, and someone pushed a small, reluctant man into the arena. The crowd's voices rose with intensity. When he was almost at the center of the amphitheater, a second gate opened, and out walked the first beast. Slowly, steadily, it circled its prey. Then another lion entered, and another, and suddenly, the lions stood still. The man looked around frantically.

The people stopped their cries. Tension mounted. Then, in a flash, the lions charged the man, each vying for a piece of juicy dinner. The crowd cheered and applauded as each piece of flesh was ripped from the man's body. This was what the crowds had been waiting for. In a matter of seconds, another Christian was devoured.

Suffering for doing
wrong, Peter said,
is a given.

As persecution against Christians began, Peter wanted to counsel, warn, and encourage those who feared for their lives. Would Rome's cruel arm reach them? Would they become some of the many believers targeted for persecution?

Peter knew about suffering. He had watched his own beloved Teacher and Master, the Son of God, suffer a cruel death of crucifixion. As Jesus' disciples spread the good news of the Savior's death, burial, and resurrection, more and more trouble erupted. Jesus' words to them were becoming reality: "In this world you will have trouble. But take heart! I have overcome the world" (John 16:33).

It's that last part that troubled them. What did it mean to "overcome the world"? They were the ones being overcome. Christians were dying for the cause of Christ! Yet Peter was telling them that suffering was really a blessing, something in which they could find joy (1 Pet. 4:13). How was that possible?

Suffering for doing wrong, Peter said, is a given. No one sympathizes with you for getting what you justly deserve. But enduring persecution for doing good, for the sake of Christ, is a different story. That's when you actually participate in Christ's sufferings and are following his example (1 Pet. 2:20-21).

But where does the blessing come in? And how can you possibly enjoy such a thing? Some of the blessings Peter said we can count on are things such as the peace of knowing trials are temporary: "After you have suffered a little while, [God] will himself restore you" (1 Pet. 5:10). I have repeatedly told my daughters that we can get through anything when we know it is only for a short period. The end may not appear to be in sight, but we can see a bright future, a positive end, with eyes of faith.

Peter included the blessing of our faith's being refined: "[Trials] have come so that your faith—of greater worth than gold, which perishes even though refined by fire—may be proved genuine" (1 Pet. 1:7). And what about the praise of God when Christ is revealed? Peter added that our suffering would result in a stronger belief and love for Christ, and an "inexpressible and glorious joy" (1 Pet. 1:8).

But Peter was not finished. What about the joy of experiencing the "Spirit of glory and of God" resting on you when someone insults you for Christ's sake (1 Pet. 4:14)? Or the promise that we will be made "firm and steadfast" by "the God of all grace" himself? (1 Pet. 5:10).

The blessings of persecution and suffering are often hidden from view. We can't always visualize the bigger picture. But even the apostle Paul, when imprisoned for his faith, encouraged Christians to think beyond their own visual screens of understanding. His fellow believers saw his prison sentence as a detriment, not a blessing. Not only that, they felt many had moved into Paul's spot and begun preaching out of "envy and rivalry." But Paul said his chains carried hidden blessings because they "served to advance the gospel." His imprisonment actually encouraged other believers to preach with more boldness and courage. The most important thing was that they preached about Christ, whether from good or selfish motives. And the whole situation made Paul happy (Phil. 1:12-14)!

> Peter and Paul agreed on what no math scholars can ever explain: in God's scheme of things, subtraction actually equals multiplication.

Peter and Paul agreed on what no math scholars can ever

explain: in God's scheme of things, subtraction actually equals multiplication. The proof? In almost every country where you find persecution, you will discover new believers mushrooming.

Jesus himself told his followers, "Blessed [happy, joyful] are those who are persecuted because of righteousness, / for theirs is the kingdom of heaven" (Matt. 5:10). And though we do not work for rewards, and our relationship with God does not depend on that, God loves to honor those who endure suffering for his sake. "Great," Jesus said, "is your reward" (Matt. 5:12).

Peter understood what he was writing about. Some historians say it was during one of Nero's bloody persecutions that Peter died. Feeling unworthy to follow in his Master's manner of death, he insisted on being crucified upside down.[9]

One day the gate will swing open wide. Millions of spectators will have gathered for the occasion. Surrounding the entire "arena" will be a host of celestial beings just waiting to join in the celebration. You will enter through the gate, feeling a bit overwhelmed, not sure what to expect. And as you walk to the center of the huge "amphitheater," the crowd rises to its feet and begins to cheer.

Your heart pounds, but not with fear. Your eyes and your ears are not tuned to the crowd. You seek Another's applause. You are listening, searching for something else. Suddenly the spectators stop. Silence. And then the King of Glory stands and begins to walk toward you.

With a voice as calming as the gentle rain but as thunderous as a million roaring lions, he speaks to you—and to you alone. His hand extends, and you rush to kneel at his feet. "Great is your reward," says the King. And you silently proclaim, *It has been worth it all.*

The crowd roars with approval. God has granted his ultimate blessing for you to enjoy for eternity.

PERSONAL TRUTH

Earthly losses are minimal in light of eternity.

PERSONAL PRAYER

Lord, you gave up everything and endured so much just to give me life. Why should I be surprised if others treat me the same way they treated you? How can I complain when suffering knocks at my door?

PERSONAL QUESTION

What has God taught you through personal suffering?

HUNGRY FOR GOD

Blessed are those who hunger
and thirst for righteousness,
for they will be filled.

—Matthew 5:6

Our people are forced to eat roots and leaves. Mothers are being forced to scrabble in the dirt to find roots, and pluck any leaves from the trees, to find some way of feeding their children! Maize is being eaten green from the stalk, meaning that it has gone by harvest time! . . . People fight with animals when looking for water."[10]

"There is food enough for all, yet hunger persists. Hunger continues to plague our world because people either do not have access to food or they cannot afford to buy the food that is available. Over 840 million people around the world receive insufficient nutrition."[11]

"Hunger and malnutrition claim one child every 5 seconds, according to U.N. statistics."[12]

These statistics and stories are real. So is hunger. And if hunger brings grief, disease, and even death, how in the world could it bring a blessing?

But Jesus wasn't talking in Matthew about malnourished bodies. He wasn't referring to impoverished spirits. When Jesus said, "Blessed [happy] are those who hunger and thirst for righteousness," he was talking about a gnawing, intense pain, but it wasn't physical. The psalmist spoke of the same longings: "As the deer pants for streams of water, / so my soul pants for you, O God. / My soul thirsts for God, for the living God. / When can I go and meet with God?" (Ps. 42:1–2).

> Freedom—and fulfillment—would come only by way of Jesus.

A man named Nicodemus went looking for something to satisfy his hunger and thirst, and his search took him on a nighttime trek. But in that hour he wasn't foraging for food in trash bins to feed his hungry body—he was craving truth. Curious, seeking answers, perhaps even intellectual information to relay to his Jewish cohorts, this noted Pharisee ruler approached Jesus at night. Why? Perhaps embarrassment, or fear. For whatever reason, Nicodemus risked danger and chose this off-the-record moment to do some soul investigation. And Jesus never disappoints the sincere seeker. He was waiting to answer Nicodemus's need.

Nicodemus recognized that something was different about this Teacher. After all, Jesus had performed miracles, a feat reserved for someone who obviously knew God. Jesus went to the heart of the Pharisee's need when he said, "No one can see the kingdom of God unless he is born again" (John 3:3).

Nicodemus was hungry for something else: an end to bondage to Rome, a time when the Jewish people would put all enemies under their thumb. *Born again?* He must have thought. *Born again? What kind of kingdom is this?* Nicodemus scratched his head and questioned the impossibility of such a birth procedure.

But Jesus was not talking about a physical birth. He went on to explain how only God could accomplish such a supernatural feat as a spiritual birth: "For God so loved the world that he gave his one and only Son, that whoever believes in him shall not perish but have eternal life" (John 3:16). That spiritual birth was the answer to Nicodemus's hunger. And his belief in Jesus as the Son of God would be the means by which that hunger was filled. Freedom—and fulfillment—would come only by way of Jesus.

Jesus ended his discussion with Nicodemus by cautioning the ruler indirectly about secret deeds and discipleship. Those who hate the light will avoid it because their dark deeds would be seen. "But whoever lives by the truth comes into the light, so that it may be seen plainly that what he has done has been done through God" (John 3:21).

How did Nicodemus receive Jesus' words? Sometime later, it was Nicodemus who tried to persuade the other Jewish rulers and Sanhedrin not to prejudge Jesus, to give him a fair hearing. That bold act brought a stabbing accusation against Nicodemus: "Are you from Galilee, too?" (John 7:52). In other words, "Nicodemus, are you a secret follower of Jesus?"

We are left to wonder until the burial of Jesus. Two wealthy men boldly stepped forward from the shadows into the light to claim Jesus' body. Both disciples on the sly until then, they instantly opened themselves up to possible persecution and Jewish excommunication. But their spiritual hunger pains had grown too intense to ignore. One of those men was Nicodemus, who brought seventy-five pounds of myrrh and aloes with which to bury Jesus in a rich man's grave (John 19:38-40).

> We do not have to search back alleys or scrabble through dirty garbage bins to fill our hunger.

A. W. Tozer writes of those "whose religious lives are marked by a growing hunger after God Himself. They are eager for spiritual realities and will not be put off with words, nor will they be content with correct 'interpretations' of truth. They are athirst for God, and they will not be satisfied till they have drunk deep at the Fountain of Living Water."[13]

There is food enough for all, yet hunger persists. We do not have to search back alleys or scrabble through dirty garbage bins to fill our hunger. Yet people are dying from spiritual starvation—because they don't know where to find food. When we approach God with empty, hungry hearts; when we are willing to admit that he is all we need; when we cry out with the soul's deepest longing, "I must have you, God, or I will die"; we won't have to beg, scratch, or fight to quench our hunger and thirst. Jesus is the spiritual food that satisfies every hunger pain.

The blessing from that kind of longing—the kind that "hungers and thirsts after righteousness"—is God's filling us with himself. Isn't it amazing that when he fills us up, we suddenly care deeply about feeding others as well—both spiritually and physically?

PERSONAL TRUTH

Only those who have experienced true hunger can appreciate the real joy of being filled.

PERSONAL PRAYER

Father, where can we go but to you? In our neediness and in our hunger, we cry out to you for the Living Manna that will always satisfy and for the River of Life that never runs dry. We are desperate for you, God!

PERSONAL QUESTION

How long has it been since you experienced true spiritual hunger?

THE REAL HERO

I will go with you.
But because of the way you are going about this,
the honor will not be yours,
for the LORD will hand Sisera over to a woman.

—Judges 4:9

He was celebrated as a hero, but when the real story was told, the truth came out. Ted Engstrom described what actually happened:

The party aboard ship was in full swing. Speeches were being made by the captain, the crew, and the guests enjoying the week-long voyage. Sitting at the head table was a seventy-year-old man who, somewhat embarrassed, was doing his best to accept the praise being poured on him.

Earlier that morning a young woman had apparently fallen overboard, and within seconds this elderly gentleman was in the cold, dark waters at her side. The woman was rescued and the elderly man became an instant hero.

When time finally came for the brave passenger to speak, the stateroom fell into a hush as he rose from his chair. He went to the microphone and, in what was probably the shortest "hero's" speech ever offered, spoke these stirring words: "I just want to know one thing—who pushed me?"[14]

Another man in Scripture, Barak, struggled with similar emotions. At that time in Israel's history, God's people were at war with neighboring tribes. After entering the promised land of Canaan under Joshua's leadership, they had failed to drive out the inhabitants of the land as God had commanded them. The danger of keeping their enemies as slaves or even next-door neighbors was that they might come to accept those nations' false gods and irreverent beliefs—and God knew it. So, when the Israelites indeed found themselves bedfellows with idolatry, God allowed them to fall into the hands of their enemy nations to get their attention (Judg. 1:27, 2:1-13). When the Israelites repented, God raised up a judge to help them.

> Instead of demonstrating immediate courage and faith, he was reluctant to the core and refused to budge at Deborah's firm push.

In this case, a woman named Deborah was a judge over Israel. An angel sent a message to this woman prophetess—one who listened to and obeyed the voice of God. Day after day, Deborah held court and judged disputes under the palm tree in her front yard in the hill country of Ephraim. Down below on the plains, a wicked commander named Sisera had cruelly oppressed the Hebrew people for twenty years. But when God called, Deborah responded with courage.

Through her, God gave the responsibility of battle with Israel's enemies to Barak, but he refused—unless she went with him. Deborah was a wife, a judge, and a strong leader with keen insight. She did not seek honor for herself. She simply relayed a message from God to Barak: go and attack Sisera and his army. Barak, however, had a yellow streak. Instead of demonstrating courage and faith, he was reluctant to the core and refused to budge at Deborah's firm push. He agreed to rally the men and go, but only if he could hide behind Deborah's skirts—er, faith. Deborah agreed but warned Barak that because of his cowardice, the honor would go not to him but to a woman.

Sisera received word that Barak was poised and ready for battle, so he took his men, in nine hundred iron chariots, and prepared to attack. It was Deborah who sounded the battle cry to Barak: "Go! This is the day the LORD has given Sisera into your hands. Has not the LORD gone ahead of you?" (Judg. 4:14).

The Lord indeed went before them and muddied the water, so to speak, to make victory impossible for Sisera. In the middle of a thunderous downpour of rain, Sisera's iron chariots bogged down, rendering his men easy targets. The Israelites routed Sisera's entire army—but Sisera got away (see Judg. 5).

When Sisera fled on foot, he found refuge in the tent of Jael, the wife of Heber the Kenite. He thought he was home safe, because Heber the Kenite maintained friendly relations with Sisera's king, Jabin.

But God always has the last word. Perhaps Sisera didn't know or had forgotten that these particular Kenites were descendants of Moses' brother-in-law. In the end, it was the courage of another woman who drove the final nail (pardon the pun) into Sisera's coffin. While Sisera slept, Jael took a simple tent peg and nailed Sisera literally to the ground. End of Sisera. And soon, the end of Jabin, the Canaanite king.

> Real courage doesn't try to take the glory for itself but recognizes that all the credit belongs to God alone.

True to God's prophecy, the honor of destroying Israel's greatest enemy went to an ordinary woman—Jael—who, just like Deborah, acted with courage in the face of oppression. And the result was forty years of peace for Israel (Judg. 5:31).

This biblical story is not just about a woman. It's about courage—and faith, and trusting the one who is stronger and greater and by whom all things are possible. Real courage doesn't try to take the glory for itself but recognizes that all the credit belongs to God alone. Following their victory, Deborah and Barak both sang a song of praise and worship to the real hero: God himself.

Has God asked you to do something for him? Perhaps you have felt like Barak at times and pleaded with God, "I can't do this alone!" Sometimes God provides the answer through someone "with skin on," as he did for Barak and for Moses, through his brother, Aaron (Exod. 4). Other times God intends for you to work alone. But even then, he is always in the wings. Throughout the Bible, God prompts and encourages his people, "Be strong, take courage!" (see Deut. 31:6, Josh. 1:9, 2 Chron. 32:7, Jer. 1:8, John 6:20). The promise usually follows: "I will be with you." And he always is.

Courage becomes a true blessing the moment we recognize that the real Hero is the one who is behind us—pushing.

PERSONAL TRUTH

Heroes are those who shrink not from duty, but from self-glory.

PERSONAL PRAYER

God, you are indeed the real Hero of my life. You are not only behind me, gently prompting; you go before me, walk beside me, and surround me daily with encouragement. How can I say thanks?

PERSONAL QUESTION

How has God been your hero?

INCORRIGIBLE ENCOURAGERS

Let us encourage one another.

—Hebrews 10:25

Born the seventh child in the early 1900s to English parents, Maria and Samuel Hansen, May experienced heartache repeatedly as a child. Her country was fighting in a world war, and she lost most of her brothers and father to the battle. May herself barely survived traumatic injuries she received when a bomb exploded near her, sending her to the hospital unconscious and bandaged from head to toe.

But May was more than a survivor. She spent her life helping others as a nurse-governess. After her husband died and her children were grown, May married a gentle man named Joe Lemke. At the time, her devotion, determination, and tender love for children had earned her the reputation of miracle worker. But it all stemmed from May's true heart: she was an incorrigible encourager.

Soon after her second marriage, May received a call asking her to take in a foster child. She agreed but soon discovered Leslie was no ordinary child.

In the movie *Seabiscuit,* when a man was asked why he kept an old, lame horse around, the man replied, "You don't throw away a whole life just 'cause he's banged up a little." That old nag ended up being instrumental in another horse's successful racing career.

Leslie, too, was "banged up a little." The six-month old infant had been born severely retarded and with cerebral palsy. His eyes were so badly damaged they had both been removed. Everyone else would have given up on this child, but not May Lemke.

> "You don't throw away a whole life just 'cause he's banged up a little."

Years passed, and May kept encouraging and loving Leslie—never giving up. It wasn't until Leslie was ten years old that May detected even some slight indication that Leslie would possibly walk one day.

May and her husband, both well into their sixties, continued their rituals of exercise, feeding, talking, and even playing musical recordings for Leslie day after day. When Leslie was thirteen, they bought a piano, and May began to play simple songs for Leslie to hear. Still, no sounds. No expression. Nothing.

But May began to pray for God to give Leslie a talent, a gift of some kind. Then one day the unimaginable happened. At age sixteen, Leslie pulled himself to the piano in his room, never having played a note. The spastic hands that usually flailed wildly began to play flawlessly Tchaikovsky's Piano Concerto no. 1.

The Lemkes soon discovered Leslie could play anything he heard. Miracles continued. Imagine his parents' surprise one day when strains of "How Great Thou Art" began to flow from Leslie's mouth!

Leslie gave concerts all over the country, singing songs of love, songs of joy, and songs about Jesus—all because one woman believed his was a life worth saving, he had a talent worth developing, and he illustrated a message that was life-changing. All because May was an encourager who believed in her son.[15]

I bet Barnabas's parents believed in him too. His name meant "Son of Encouragement," and Barnabas lived up to it (Acts 4:36). One day Barnabas sold a field and donated the money to the apostles to encourage and help new believers (Acts 4:36). Later when a man named Saul, a former persecutor of Christians, suddenly turned into a fiery evangelist, the disciples in Jerusalem questioned his authenticity. What if Saul-turned-Paul was really out to kill them? But Barnabas, the "Son of Encouragement," heard Paul's testimony and had witnessed his fearless preaching in Damascus. So Barnabas stood up for Paul. After all, you don't discard a life just because it's been banged up a little.

Time passed, and Jewish believers scattered after an early Christian, Stephen, was martyred (Acts 7). Eventually, some began sharing their faith not only with Jews, but also with the Greeks. New believers need encouragement, so the church at Jerusalem sent Barnabas—"a good man, full of the Holy Spirit and faith" (Acts 11:24). Barnabas adopted the baby Christians at Antioch and nursed them in their newfound faith. As the people and work grew, Barnabas asked Paul to join him. What a great team (Acts 11:26)!

The encourager may begin in the front seat, but he eventually retreats to his rightful place in the background. At some point after Paul and Barnabas had traveled together, Paul emerged as the leader. They even split over a dispute and separated— perhaps because a true encourager's instincts and sense of fairness always demand loyalty. Barnabas wanted to take his cousin John Mark on a second missionary journey with Paul. But John Mark had deserted them once before, and Paul said, "No way!" (Acts 15:36–39).

> The encourager may begin in the front seat, but he eventually retreats to his rightful place in the background.

Barnabas faded into the background, as many encouragers do. There are always orphans to adopt, lives that have been banged up, and hungry hearts that need spiritual encouragement. Encouragers don't look for honors but the results of their encouragement, like the works of Barnabas, are unmistakable. Later as Paul wrote from prison encouraging another beloved son of the faith, he requested that Timothy bring John Mark to see Paul, "because he is helpful to me in my ministry" (2 Tim. 4:11). My guess is that Barnabas and Paul also reunited in spirit, and each continued in the work God called him to do.

William Barclay says,

> One of the highest of human duties is the duty of encouragement. . . .
> It is easy to laugh at men's ideals; it is easy to pour cold water on their
> enthusiasm; it is easy to discourage others. The world is full of
> discouragers. We have a Christian duty to encourage one another.
> Many a time a word of praise of thanks or appreciation or cheer has
> kept a man on his feet. Blessed is the man who speaks such a word.[16]

Blessed indeed. But who receives the greatest blessing? Leslie Lemke, Paul, John Mark, and that lame horse, would no doubt all agree that they owed their very lives and usefulness to the ones who encouraged them. Where would they have been if friends had not believed in them, stood by their sides, and visualized success for their lives? Where would we be?

We who have been "banged up a little" know the answer to that question. For some of us, it may have made the difference between a glue factory and a winning race, so to speak, an orphanage or a loving home, prison or freedom, life or death.

But if we could hear again from Barnabas, he would probably humbly disagree on who was the most blessed. True encouragers have learned from the God of encouragement himself: it is always more blessed to give than to receive.

PERSONAL TRUTH

Speak words of life; someone may be dying to hear them.

PERSONAL PRAYER

Lord, where would I be without those who have blessed me with their encouragement, their comfort, and their support? And where would I be if you had not encouraged my heart, again and again? Help me not only to enjoy this blessing of encouragement but to be an encourager as well.

PERSONAL QUESTION

Have you encouraged anyone today?

WHEN YOU'VE SAID GOOD-BYE
TO YOUR DREAMS

So now I give him to the LORD.
For his whole life he will be given over to the LORD.

—1 Samuel 1:28

It was time. No more dimpled smiles, no more clinging hugs, no more shrieks of laughter to warm the heart. The caseworker had prepared her for this moment, but Laura still had difficulty facing it. "Foster children are just that," the woman had emphasized. "They are yours to foster and nourish for a short time—only until we can make permanent arrangements."

But the heart and the head don't always agree. Emotions ran rampant, and tears flowed freely as Laura placed the toddler's small body in the arms of the caseworker. The woman assured Laura she could have more foster children. But this was Laura's first foster child, and long years had passed since her own children had left her maternal nest. A few weeks had turned into several months. Now she had formed an emotional attachment to the child.

Laura had rearranged her whole life around this little one—adjusting to early morning feedings, diaper bags, and messy floors. Colorful toys, some still unopened, filled every corner of the house. She had even purchased a secondhand rocker, where she spent many sleepless nights trying to calm a colicky infant. How could Laura bear the emptiness to follow? And what child could fill the hole in her heart like this one?

Perhaps Hannah experienced similar feelings. Hannah, though, had always been barren. Time after time, she accompanied her husband, Elkanah, to the temple in Shiloh. Year after year she listened to the taunts of her rival, Peninnah, who had been blessed with children. And her pain grew only more intense.

> She had just said good-bye to the most important dream of her heart!

One day Hannah could take it no longer. So great was her distress, she could not eat. Hannah wept as if her heart would break. Through her tears, the Bible says, she prayed a silent vow: that if God would grant her a son, she would give that child to God all his life (1 Sam. 1:11).

Eli the priest saw Hannah's lips moving but heard no sound. His hasty accusation wounded Hannah's heart even more: he assumed she was drunk. Did no one understand Hannah's grief?

God did. And so did Eli after Hannah explained the reason for her tears. Eli dismissed the barren mother with God's blessing, believing with her that she would receive her request.

The following year Hannah gave birth to a beautiful son. Dimpled cheeks, clinging hugs, and shrieks of laughter from her growing child replaced Hannah's bitterness with joy. Midnight feedings, sleepless nights, and toys littered in every corner—Hannah didn't seem to mind. Time passed, and Hannah stayed home for a while to nurse their baby. Months seemed like minutes.

Then one day, it was time. The entire family made its way to the temple at Shiloh. After offering the required sacrifice, Hannah gathered little Samuel in her arms for one last hug, then gave her own personal offering: she kept her promise to God and surrendered her child to Eli the priest for the Lord's work (1 Sam. 1:28).

Then Hannah heaved a sigh and wept bitterly. Right? Wrong. The next chapter records another of Hannah's prayers—and it is anything but sad. The first sounds from her mouth are words of joy:

> My heart rejoices in the LORD;
>> in the LORD my horn is lifted high.
> My mouth boasts over my enemies,
>> for I delight in your deliverance.
> There is no one holy like the LORD;
>> there is no one besides you;
> there is no Rock like our God. (1 Samuel 2:1–2)

How could Hannah be so happy? She had just said good-bye to the most important dream of her heart! She had just relinquished her son to the care of someone else! And Eli had rebellious sons of his own—how could he raise someone else's child when he couldn't even control his own teenagers (1 Sam. 2:12–17)? How would Hannah cope with seeing her son only once a year when she visited the temple (1 Sam. 2:19–20)?

Hannah would not witness all of her son's progress firsthand. What mother doesn't love to boast of her children's achievements? Tucked inside forgotten drawers or stashed in bulging boxes are the faded ribbons of former glory days. Each picture or award announces its own story—and every mother has one to tell, if you ask her.

> When Hannah surrendered her son, she relinquished her paints and canvas as well.

But it's not just what her children *do* that makes a mother love them. It's who they are, and, if they are grown, who they have become. Godly character is something she wants desperately to build into their lives. A mother may feel unskilled and overwhelmed as she looks at her raw materials and endless tasks. But when she sees the bigger picture, she will understand that successful motherhood is not about achieving but believing—believing that the one to whom she entrusts her children will complete the work he has started. While she is given the paints, God remains the Artist. And he will complete the masterpiece in his own time.

When Hannah surrendered her son, she relinquished her paints and canvas as well. But her true joy came in knowing that when she decided to *resign* her dreams to God, he was then free to *design* a dream far better than she could ever hope or imagine. God honored Hannah's selfless act. The Bible says God blessed Hannah with three more sons and two daughters (1 Sam. 2:21).

Samuel himself, the product of Hannah's dream and sacrifice, "grew up in the presence of the LORD" and became a prophet with godly character—the one chosen to anoint King David (1 Sam. 2:21).

Mirroring God's heart, Samuel once said to a disobedient king, "To obey is better than sacrifice" (1 Sam. 15:22). Evidently, Samuel had learned that truth early in life—because his mother, Hannah, understood from God the deeper meaning of obedience. She could have disobeyed and refused to honor her vow to God. Instead, with her life she painted a picture of the place, the value—and the joyful blessing—of both obedience and surrender.

PERSONAL TRUTH

God's dreams are always bigger—and better—than ours.

PERSONAL PRAYER

Lord, forgive me for clinging too tightly to my own dreams. Help me to relinquish the most treasured desires of my heart. I trust you to sift through them all and give back only what will honor you the most.

PERSONAL QUESTION

Has God asked you to surrender any dreams lately?

THE PASSION OF PURPOSE

For to me, to live is Christ.

—Philippians 1:21

Thanks to Rick Warren's book, *The Purpose-Driven Life,* thousands of people have understood a greater purpose for their lives. Rick encouraged readers: "If you want to know why you were placed on this planet, you must begin with God. You were born *by* his purpose and *for* his purpose."[17]

The apostle Paul said the same thing almost two thousand years ago: "It's in Christ that we find out who we are and what we are living for. Long before we first heard of Christ, and got our hopes up, he had his eye on us, had designs on us for glorious living, part of the overall purpose he is working out in everything and everyone" (Eph. 1:11 MSG).

For some, discovering their purpose is a chore. To others, it's a lifelong blessing. Paul fits the latter. Before Paul met Christ, he had one driving purpose: to destroy Christians. But when he encountered the living presence of Christ, Paul suddenly had a new passion.

Paul set out to fulfill his newfound purpose by declaring his faith everywhere he went. He started new churches, encouraged believers and became a zealous missionary for Christ. Shipwrecks, beatings, snakebites, and imprisonments only strengthened Paul's passion and purpose. Letter after letter in the Bible's New

Testament—some of which Paul wrote from a prison cell—bears Paul's signature and testifies to his newfound blessing of purpose. His very reason for living was Christ: to know him, to worship him, to serve him, and to live for him alone. Paul wrote, "I run straight to the goal with purpose in every step" (1 Cor. 9:26 NLT).

> Purpose is what drags a pain-riddled body, one leg at a time, to answer the call for something greater than himself.

Did Paul accomplish his God-given purpose? Absolutely. Nearing his death, Paul said to his disciple Timothy, "This is the only race worth running. I've run hard right to the finish, believed all the way. All that's left now is the shouting—God's applause!" (2 Tim. 4:7–8 MSG).

I've spent some time thinking about this God-given thing called *purpose*—and about the passion that so completely consumed Paul and a host of other biblical and contemporary characters. What does the passion and the blessing of purpose feel and look and act like? I've discovered it's not at all what I thought; and it's more than I thought.

It's the breath of God spurring you on when you want to quit, a fire in the bones, like Jeremiah's, that cannot be quenched (Jer. 20:9)—or the sweet songs from the psalmist David that refuse to be silenced.

Purpose is what drags a pain-riddled body, one leg at a time, to answer the call for something greater than himself: "Here am I! Send me. Please send me!" It's the heart bathed with grace and gratitude—the face turned like flint toward something intangible, and more powerful than can be explained. It's the canning of *I can'ts* and the opening of *I can's*.

Purpose is different, yet the same for everyone. As I look back over my life, I see God revealed his purpose in the most unlikely places, scattering his markers for me to find. These pieces of my life seemed like unpolished gems at the time, but with age and care they now shine like diamonds.

I found purpose in the gentle and steadfast heart of a man in whom I could trust implicitly. It hovered in a simple kitchen, where even burnt, pitiful offerings turned to gratefully received, plentiful feasts. I discovered it in the soft lullabies of a too-young mom caressing her infant in the predawn hours. In Mexico, I felt it in the shivering body of a young waif wrapped in the folds of my warm coat, and I experienced it in the affection of Peruvian men, women, and children sacrificing their all for my comfort.

The passion welled up in my heart each time I introduced others to his Words, and to the joys of knowing my Creator for themselves. And even in the face of a thousand writing rejections, I felt its wind on my back and its hand clasped in mine, always whispering my name softly. I embraced its truths and cried its tears as I watched my children pass through my life like sifted flour.

I found the greatest example of purpose and passion in the Lord Jesus himself. "For I have come down from heaven not to do my will but to do the will of him who sent me" (John 6:38). Jesus accomplished that purpose in his death on the cross. His dying words said it all: "It is finished" (John 19:30).

> God instills the passion—and the purpose—to bring him glory any way he chooses.

To know that God created us for his purpose is a joyful blessing in itself. And to discover his purpose in the ordinary details of life is thrilling. But realizing the uniqueness of how God plays out his individual purpose in us is absolutely exhilarating. I love knowing that God has some specialized tasks with my name on them.

I have come to realize that like a grand orchestra leader, my

Creator has been conducting the symphony of my life all along. It came as a whisper from heaven: "Add my beauty; write my words." No fiery tongs from an angel's hand (Isa. 6:6). No burning bush on the mountainside (Exod. 3:2–6). No blinding light from a darkened sky (Acts 9:3). Just a persistent whisper. For me, writing had yielded only temporal rewards. But one day that changed. Like Eric Liddell in *Chariots of Fire* who admitted, "When I run, I feel God's pleasure," my heart's passion and purpose became "When I write for him, I see God's smile."

My words will probably never change a heart or move a nation—but his words, dressed in the clothing from heaven's wardrobe, can leap over walls of hatred, prejudice, despair, and confusion. His words, wrapped around the microphone of my pen, can encourage, teach, and love. They can spur others to find and be and do greater things than I could ever imagine. In other words, when I write about God, I have the distinct privilege of encouraging others to know, to love, and to hunger for the one who writes purpose on every life.

We have so many choices in life, so many good things that call our names. But whatever God writes your name on will always bring you the most joy and fulfillment as well as accomplish the most for him. God instills the passion—and the purpose—to bring him glory any way he chooses. And for us to be effective, he *must* be the source of our passion. The real blessing of fulfilling our unique, God-designed purpose is to be able to share one day in that throng of witnesses gathered around God's throne in heaven and say, as Paul did, "I have finished the race, I have kept the faith" (2 Tim. 4:7).

All that's left then will be the shouting—God's applause.

PERSONAL TRUTH

Whatever you do, do it for God's applause.

PERSONAL PRAYER

Lord, unless you write the words, I have nothing to say. Unless you compose the song, there will be no music. Thank you for giving me a purpose—and the passion to accomplish it for you.

PERSONAL QUESTION

What are you doing that has God's signature on it?

THE THRILL OF ADVENTURE

I do not have time to tell about [those] . . .
who through faith conquered kingdoms, . . .
who shut the mouths of lions, quenched the fury of the flames,
and escaped the edge of the sword;
whose weakness was turned to strength.

—Hebrews 11:32–34

I am amazed when I hear others describe the Christian life this way: "It's so boring! Where's the adventure?"

That's when I turn to *Webster's*. What is adventure, anyway? It is literally "a happening." But there's more: "the encountering of danger; exciting and dangerous undertaking; an unusual, stirring experience, often of a romantic nature."[18]

Is Christianity boring? Check into the following headlines and decide for yourself:

Man Sees Burning Bush That Will Not Extinguish
Red Sea Rolls Up Like a Carpet as Millions Walk Through to
    Dry Land
Giant Killed by an Ordinary Teen's Slingshot
Jewish Queen Saves Her People from Annihilation
Three Men Survive Blazing Furnace Without a Singe
Man Raised from the Dead After Four Days
City Walls Mysteriously Crumble

Man Swallowed Alive by Fish Lives to Tell About It
Man of God Disappears into the Heavens on a Chariot of Fire

These are not exaggerated fabrications of a tabloid magazine. They are actual "happenings"—God-adventures in the Bible. And they hardly sound boring.

> Life with God *will* involve the "encountering of danger," an "exciting and dangerous undertaking," and/or an "unusual, stirring experience, often of a romantic nature."

The one who decides to enter the kingdom of God as a Christ-one, a believer and follower of the Lord Jesus Christ, may not make headlines such as these, but every deeply committed Christian can bank on this: life with God *will* involve the "encountering of danger," an "exciting and dangerous undertaking," and/or "an unusual, stirring experience, often of a romantic nature."

John Eldredge says, "Adventure, with all its requisite danger and wildness, is a deeply spiritual longing written into the soul of man." He continues, "Adventure requires something of us, puts us to the test. Though we may fear the test, at the same time we yearn to be tested, to discover that we have what it takes."[19]

While men welcome an adventure to live, likewise, Eldredge says, "every woman wants an adventure to share." Perhaps that's what drew Abraham and Sarah into their great adventure together with God. He followed wherever God led him, and to her credit, Sarah rarely questioned her man's integrity or daring spirit. Not even when, early in his journey, Abraham forgot about being a hero to his beautiful wife—what Eldredge says is part of every true "wild at heart" man.[20]

Adventure usually requires a test involving selfish wills, nature, insurmountable odds or fearful circumstances. Perhaps it was a combination of these that led Abraham to fail one of his first real tests.

Genesis 12 says a famine forced Abraham (then called Abram) to move into Egypt, and fear crowded out his sense of duty to his wife, Sarah (then called Sarai). He praised Sarah for her beauty; score one point. But then through faulty reasoning he said, "When the Egyptians see you, they will say, 'This is his wife.' Then they will kill me but will let you live." So he asked Sarah to lie for him—or at least tell a half-truth. Same thing. " 'Say you are my sister, so that I will be treated well for your sake and my life will be spared because of you' " (vv. 12–13).

Whoa! There's something wrong with this picture. True, Sarah was his half-sister (Gen. 20:12). But who's rescuing whom here? Some wild man! Sarah was to risk *her* life so *he* would be treated well; how would *she* be treated? Abraham was asking Sarah to rescue him from a danger that might not have even existed.

But a gracious God intervened. While Pharaoh did treat Abraham well for Sarah's sake, he also took Sarah to his palace. Consequently God, who is the ultimate "wild at heart" rescuer, inflicted Pharaoh's entire household with disease. Pharaoh got the picture and sent Abraham away—with his wife (Gen. 12:17–19).

You would think Abraham learned his lesson. Over his long life, Abraham had been given the promise of a son, had seen God destroy Sodom and Gomorrah, and had talked with God and angels on numerous occasions (Gen. 17–19). But it's the same story, second verse. Abraham pretended Sarah again was his sister. She was once more taken to join a king's harem. And once more, God delivered Sarah from the hands of a strange king before anyone had time to think about touching her (Gen. 20:1–20).

> Our adventure with God never ends.

In spite of Abraham's weaknesses, God kept drawing Abe's heart into his own, with the spirit of romance and adventure. And at age one hundred, Abraham became a father at last—but not just any dad. God made him the father of all nations (Gen. 22:17–18).

Eldredge says, "If a man is ever to find out who he is and what he is here for, he has got to take that journey for himself."[21] Abraham took the journey, and he found that life was worth living. And he discovered the true blessing of his God-adventures.

As with Abraham, our adventure with God never ends: "God, who got you started in this spiritual adventure, shares with us the life of his Son and our Master Jesus. He will never give up on you. Never forget that" (1 Cor. 1:9 MSG). Henry Blackaby says, "When God is about to do something through you, He has to get you from where you are to where He is."[22] That's what he did for Abraham. That's what he wants to do for us. That's where the blessing of adventure lies.

Because wherever God is, rest assured, adventure will surely follow.

Personal Truth

The best adventures are those God designs especially for you.

Personal Prayer

Lord, thank you for every adventure you have brought into my life. As I look back over the years, I can see how your hand was in each one of them, guiding, teaching, but most of all, loving me. I can't wait to experience the adventures still waiting for me.

Personal Question

What has been your most exciting God-adventure so far?

THE CRUMBS OF GREAT FAITH

Then Jesus answered, "Woman, you have great faith!
Your request is granted."
And her daughter was healed from that very hour.

—Matthew 15:28

Few football players know the power of persistence and determination like Dan "Rudy" Ruettiger. Based on his life, the classic movie *Rudy* tells the story of a young man who dreamed of wearing the jersey and helmet of his favorite team. Rudy wanted to play football at Notre Dame.

One of fourteen children, Rudy was small, plain, and from a lower-middle-class family that couldn't afford such luxuries. He was like a little dog wanting to perform in a circle of stately lions. His father expected Rudy to work in the same steel mill he had worked in all of his life. The odds were not in Rudy's favor.

Rudy tried to convince Notre Dame's administration, but the school denied his request to attend. Rudy ate football, dreamed football, and lived football, twenty-four hours a day. At the age of twenty-three, Ruettiger enrolled in Holy Cross Junior College in South Bend, Indiana, and worked as a groundskeeper at Notre Dame's Knute Rockne Stadium. He studied hard, but his grades were not good enough to get him in Notre Dame.

But Rudy wouldn't give up. After each semester, he applied

again to Notre Dame. Each time, a letter arrived dashing Rudy's dreams. *Sorry, not good enough.*

Rudy only studied harder. Then one day, after his familiar trip to the mailbox he sat down, preparing for yet another rejection. This time was different. A huge grin broke out on his face. *Yes!* He was going to Notre Dame.

Persistence had paid off for Rudy.

But that was only half the challenge. Could he make the team? Bloodied, ridiculed, and exhausted, Rudy tried out like a mad man. Finally, he won a place as a practice player for two years, even though he was not allowed to suit up. But he had so endeared himself to the players because of his guts and persistence that on the night before the last game, every player on the newly chosen team walked into the coach's office and offered to trade in his jersey—to give up his place—to make room for Rudy. No one had ever seen such determination as this young man displayed.

The coach relented, and the first time Rudy ran through the Notre Dame goalposts onto the field the next day, he thought he would burst with pride. Though Rudy's skills and size rated him only a benchwarmer, with only a few minutes left in the last game a chant broke out in the stands: "Ru-dy! Ru-dy! Ru-dy! Ru-dy!" It grew louder and louder until finally the coach sent Rudy in.

Rudy scored no touchdowns, and he made only one tackle. But that wasn't what counted to Rudy. He played! Rudy was a bona fide Notre Dame football player. His lifelong dream had come true. Persistence had paid off for Rudy.

This humble young man had not feasted on steak from the winner's table. At best, he had been tossed a few crumbs—a chance to fulfill, in a small way, a lifelong dream. But for a man like Rudy, it was enough.

The Bible talks about a woman with similar persistence. Her dream was different, but like Rudy, she never wavered in her determination. She approached Jesus, who had just retreated to the region of Tyre and Sidon with his disciples. This mother was a descendant of the immoral Canaanites.[23] Still, in one sense, she was no different from any Jewish mother who just wanted a happy, normal child. But something had gone terribly wrong.

Demon possession turned normal children into wild animals. Untamed, unkempt, thrashing uncontrollably, the daughter turned her mother's dream into a nightmare. So she turned to the only hope she could find: Jesus. Everywhere Jesus and the disciples stepped, this woman followed behind them, crying out repeatedly, "Lord, Son of David, have mercy on me!" (Matt. 15:22).

The disciples urged Jesus to send this annoying woman away. Maybe she made them uncomfortable; positionally, no Gentile had the right to address Jesus the way she did—as the Lord, the son of David. Or maybe they had no clue how to help her. But ignoring the woman did not discourage her. For a while, Jesus did nothing.

Finally, Jesus spoke, reminding his disciples that his mission and message were for only the lost Jewish people. But the woman, begging on her knees, kept pleading. She finally approached Jesus and kneeled before him.

Jesus took an understandable position and tried to explain it to the woman, testing her faith. "It is not right to take the children's bread and toss it to their dogs" (Matt. 15:26).

Everyone knew the connotation of the word "dogs." It was not a nice word. The streets were filled with mangy mongrels, stray canines who scavenged for food, even dead bodies if they could get to them. In fact, the Jewish people used this unbecoming term for the Gentiles. But Jesus was not using the word for that kind of animal. The word Jesus used was for little pet dogs. William MacDonald says Jesus was asking, "Would she acknowledge her unworthiness to receive the least of His mercies?"[24]

> God-given dreams can come true.

The Canaanite woman did so heartily. She was not too proud to admit her complete inadequacy and unworthiness as a Gentile—a little dog under the table. But she spoke to Jesus on the basis of being one of his simple, undeserving creatures: "Even the dogs eat the crumbs that fall from their masters' table" (Matt. 15:27).

And in that split second, Jesus recognized the crumbs of great faith. He had just left a host of unbelieving Jewish "children" who cared more about the meaty rules and traditions of men than about true belief in the life-changing power of Christ. He granted the woman's request. She saw a dream fulfilled and her daughter's life healed.

The blessing of true, persistent faith? God-given dreams can come true. And when Jesus blesses them, even crumbs turn into a sumptuous feast. To the curious onlooker, those crumbs could never fill an empty stomach. But the one who receives them knows they are enough to fill a hollow heart for a lifetime.

Personal Truth

Crumbs from the Master's table are better than steak from the finest restaurant.

Personal Prayer

Lord, forgive us for giving up too quickly. Teach us persistent faith, that we might pursue you with all of our hearts. We are so hungry, Lord. We are not worthy even of the crumbs of your grace, and yet you fed us with the best heaven had to offer when you gave your life for us all. In you, all our dreams are fulfilled.

Personal Question

Where do you eat your meals?

A Matter of Perspective

Whom have I in heaven but you?
  And earth has nothing I desire besides you.
My flesh and my heart may fail,
  but God is the strength of my heart
and my portion forever.

—Psalm 73:25–26

Reverend Smith trudged back home, a defeated man. For twenty years he had poured out his life, his tears, his heart on the mission field—for what? In all that time, only a handful of natives ever attended his services. His one convert—a leader in his community—was ousted and put to death.

No one cared about his God. The people still clung to age-old traditions and superstitions. The wealthy, proud, and indulgent controlled the government and the people, and every attempt to teach wisdom, integrity, and love in such a hostile environment had only escalated the tension in his community.

Reverend Smith spoke of God and his love. But where was God now? The missionary had been ridiculed, imprisoned, and re-leased, and now he and his wife had just said good-bye forever to their own child. Reports said their son had been caught in a rebels' crossfire. They had accidentally killed his child.

An accident? Smith wondered, *If God is truly who he says he is, where is God in all this? Why would God allow this to happen? Why didn't he do something to stop it?* Reverend Smith wanted one last opportunity, in preaching his own child's funeral, to tell the people that God loved them. But no one had come. So he preached to the wind, and to his own bitter heart.

This was the last straw for Reverend Smith. If nothing else was going to change, *he* would. He would pack up and leave. He told the people that he would be on a plane within twenty-four hours—gone. Ministry ended.

> Someday, truth will prevail. Good will come.

Just before heading home, Reverend Smith took one last trip to a familiar shelter. Here, each morning for twenty years, he had poured out his heart to God, asking him to do great things in the hearts of these people.

With a heavy sigh, Reverend Smith dropped to his knees and began to weep uncontrollably. Minutes, then hours passed. Still he wept: "It's not fair! God, where are you? Why don't you answer?"

Reverend Smith felt a touch on his shoulder, then another. Shuffling footsteps, awkward coughs, and then a chorus of moans began, first softly, then louder and louder. Reverend Smith turned around and gasped. A score of native families—men, women, and children snaked in a line through the bushy path as far as the eye could see—all on their knees, crying out in their own language.

The missionary turned to a familiar face behind him and asked, "What are you doing? Why are you here?"

The leader rose to his feet, and a silence fell over the entire crowd. "We heard you at the funeral of your child. We were in the bushes. We have listened to you for twenty years. Your voice carried on the wind, and even though you could not see us, we were there, listening."

"But what are you doing here now?" Reverend Smith asked.

"We are asking your God to convince you to stay. You are our only hope. We do not want you to leave. We know what really happened to your son. We watched him as he tried to convince the rebels to leave. He tried to tell them about your God. He had a big heart—like you. But they killed him because your son's words angered them. It was not right. We were afraid to tell you—afraid for our own lives.

"Someday, truth will prevail. Good will come. But we feel your pain. And we are ready to tell you we will risk our lives for your God. We no longer fear the rebels. Please, stay. Teach us. We will hear. And if necessary, we will die for our God—as your son died for his."

The story is not as unlikely as it may sound. Ask any missionary who has served on a difficult field. In reality, some may serve God for years and finally see a breakthrough, as in this fictional account. But what if the natives had never turned to God? How could the missionary's perspective have changed? Others may work for a lifetime but never see the rewards of their labor this side of heaven—men like Asaph. But Asaph learned a secret that the fictional Reverend Smith needed to know early on.

Asaph, the writer of Psalm 73, could have written in the twentieth century. He saw the wealthy amassing riches, profaning heaven, living unpunished in pride and indulgence, while the righteous seemed to suffer unjustly. The wicked around him apparently endured no struggles, lived in good health, and pursued evil without any conscience. Questioning his own standards and the apparent lack of God's judgment, he felt used, angry, and envious. Had he kept a pure heart in vain?

He reminded God of his plight as he described in vivid detail the ungodly actions and attitudes of those around him (Ps. 73:2–16). Trying to understand this apparent imbalance only deepened his depression. Hope began to drain away his energies like hot desert winds.

Until, that is, Asaph entered the sanctuary of God. And once he stepped on that hallowed ground, Asaph saw a picture of the future: scenes of sudden destruction aimed at those who had given no thought to God or his ways. The tables had turned. God had not forgotten him after all. He would take care of those who pursued injustice. One day they would face their punishment. Asaph quickly acknowledged his ignorance and bitterness toward God. His perspective changed, and God renewed his hope and strength (Ps. 73:17–28).

> Whenever we enter the sanctuary of God's holy presence, no matter when or where, we are never the same again.

Asaph understood the need to know God intimately and to maintain fellowship at all costs. He immediately reaffirmed his love for God and his desire for God's personal presence daily.

Once we enter the sanctuary of God's holy presence, we are never the same. God's purposes emerge again as he strips away our fleshly layers so we can see the true object of our affection. We are suddenly aware of the fragility of life and our own weaknesses and hopelessness apart from him. And in the midst of earth's injustices, God restores our hope and affirms that he will be our strength forever. In the presence of God, not even failing health depresses. Nothing seems to matter then—except him.

Blessed indeed is the one who can see with true godly perspective.

PERSONAL TRUTH

To know God better, enter the sanctuary of God's presence daily.

PERSONAL PRAYER

Lord, I want to know you—deeply, intimately. Peel away the layers of my heart so I can embrace you with my core being. Strip the scales from my eyes that I might receive your blessing of perspective. You are my portion, my strength, forever!

PERSONAL QUESTION

When do you have the most difficult time keeping proper perspective?

PEACEMAKING 101

Blessed are the peacemakers,
for they will be called sons of God.

—Matthew 5:9

It happens all the time. Someone in a church business meeting objects: "The carpet should be green—not blue." Another asks, "How much is it going to cost? Well, that's too much!" A third argues, "Who's on the committee, anyway? We don't need to be spending money on such trivial things."

Trivial indeed. But by the time the dust settles on the carpet, the church is facing a dilemma. The factions can't agree. Unity has been sacrificed for personal preferences. And the church is about to split.

No pastor wants to walk into a situation like that and play peacemaker, yet that scenario seems mild compared to what a young man faced almost two thousand years ago. Titus, whom Paul called his "true son in our common faith," was the man for the job (Titus 1:4).

Earlier in Paul's ministry, he had taken Titus, a Greek and a Gentile, with him to Jerusalem. There, Titus witnessed firsthand the trouble that can brew when two strong leaders—Paul and Peter—fail to agree. Paul was concerned that the Jews were setting up their own standards for being made right with God. With Titus standing before him as an object lesson, Paul warned the other leaders they were trying to rewrite the rules for peace with God instead of making peace with each other.

The outcome of that peacemaking effort was good. They ultimately agreed that Jews and Gentiles both became new creations when they placed their faith in Christ (see Galatians 2, Acts 15).

Titus's on-the-job training netted him several peacemaking assignments of his own. And the place where he was serving had deeper problems than what color of carpet the church would buy.

Unity has been sacrificed for personal preferences.

The island of Crete was populated by five ethnic groups—which could create problems of its own if they were not open-minded.[25] What a great place to pastor! Can you imagine God calling you to a congregation filled with "many rebellious people, mere talkers and deceivers, especially those of the circumcision group. . . . Even one of their own prophets has said, 'Cretans are always liars, evil brutes, lazy gluttons'" (Titus 1:10, 12)?

Against this backdrop, Paul instructed Titus to weed out the false teachers and find some strong spiritual leaders in the churches on this island. He encouraged Titus to teach women how to be reverent, godly, and pure and reminded every believer, young and old alike, to learn respect for authority and to be humble, peaceable, and considerate.

But perhaps the greatest challenge for Titus was to avoid foolish nit-picking about the law. The instruction for a divisive troublemaker was clear: warn twice, but three strikes and he's out. "After that, have nothing to do with him" (Titus 3:10).

No small task for a young peacemaker. Sometimes, being a peacemaker is not any fun. What if some hothead decided to land a hard right on his jaw? What if the church decided to split? How would he convince them to straighten up and fly right?

Several years ago my husband, Larry, and I were leading a marriage enrichment weekend in our church. We could tell one particular couple was experiencing some tension. After the retreat, they ultimately agreed they needed counseling.

During that process, much hostility and anger rose to the surface. Larry's peacemaking efforts were anything but pleasant, and he always felt a little beat-up afterwards. But gradually, as the weeks passed, the couples' countenances began to change. Their chairs moved closer together, and they held hands when they prayed. Larry watched that couple make peace and rekindle the love they had for each other. What a joy!

Larry left those sessions pumped up. I remember when he came home one day and gave me a big hug and an extra-passionate kiss. My suspicions were true: "You've been doing marriage counseling, haven't you?"

Jesus said, "Blessed [happy] are the peacemakers." Well, given the fact that peacemaking is difficult, and it requires so much strength, who would want the job, anyway? And what are the qualifications?

Whatever they are, Paul obviously thought Titus has the right stuff. Paul seemed to suggest: "Be an example of doing good and teach with authority, yet with integrity in such a way that no one can point a finger at you and say, 'Gotcha!' And remember your past—that at one point, you, too, were anything but a peacemaker: foolish, deceived, and at odds with others" (see Titus 2–3).

> God gives us the privilege—and blessing—of being peacemakers for him.

What, then, made the difference in Titus's behavior? And what gave him the authority and believability that these people would buy into his advice, living in peace with God and one another? Perhaps that difference can best be explained by missionary-anthropologist Don Richardson as he relates how God brought peace to the tribal peoples in New Guinea:

The Sawi people were a violent society of headhunters who practiced cannibalism and extolled craftiness. Yet their corrupt culture contained a mysterious custom that ultimately served as a key to their redemption. When two Sawi groups were locked in conflict, there was a way to break the pattern of treachery. A Sawi father could offer his son to the other group as a "Peace Child." The other group would receive and raise the child. As long as the Peace Child lived, past, present, and even future grievances were considered resolved. This remarkable custom of the Peace Child ultimately opened the way for the Sawi people to understand and embrace the gospel.[26]

That sort of puts the carpet color dilemma in its proper perspective, don't you think? Because of God's ultimate love for us, he sent his own Peace Child to bring two "warring" factions together: God and man. The receiver of that Peace Child would make a home in his heart for the child. And as long as that Peace Child lived, past, present, and even future grievances were considered resolved. God calls that *forgiveness*.

Titus had experienced that forgiveness and changed life. He had received God's own Peace Child into his heart. This was Titus's real message. Because of Jesus, the Peace Child who lived, died, and was resurrected, we, too, can find peace and a right relationship with God—past, present, and future. Then God gives us the privilege—and blessing—of being peacemakers for him. It brings us right into the family business (2 Cor. 5:18-21).

Those peacemakers are the true sons of faith—the ones Jesus calls "sons of God"—and that's a reason to feel blessed indeed.

Personal Truth

In order to make peace, you must have peace.

PERSONAL PRAYER

Jesus, thank you for being my Peace and for making a way for me to have peace with God. Help me to honor you well in this family business of peacemaking.

PERSONAL QUESTION

Have you been on any peacekeeping missions lately?

WORK HAPPIER, NOT HARDER

To accept his lot and be happy in his work—
this is a gift of God.
He seldom reflects on the days of his life,
because God keeps him occupied with gladness of heart.

—Ecclesiastes 5:19-20

To love what you do and feel that it matters, how could anything be more fun?"[27] Obviously the woman who said that, Katherine Graham, believed that our work can and should be a blessing. I agree. But sometimes it takes hindsight to arrive at that conclusion. At least it did for a king named Solomon.

He was named as one of the wealthiest and wisest of men who ever lived (1 Kings 4:30-31, 10:23). Yet Solomon's writings did not always reflect the joy of his work. In the book of Ecclesiastes, at times he revealed a glimpse of joy in his work—like the exhilarating sights from the top of the roller coaster—then he descended again to the valley of reality:

> *My heart took delight in all my work,*
> *and this was the reward for all my labor.*
> *Yet when I surveyed all that my hands had done*
> *and what I had toiled to achieve,*
> *everything was meaningless, a chasing after the wind;*
> *nothing was gained under the sun. (Ecclesiastes 2:10–11)*

Meaningless! Meaningless! . . .
Utterly meaningless!
Everything is meaningless.
(Ecclesiastes 1:2)

As his journals made the twists and bends along with the roller-coaster ride, he hit a bump that suddenly threw him into the pits: "What does a man get for all the toil and anxious striving with which he labors under the sun? All his days his work is pain and grief; even at night his mind does not rest" (Eccles. 2:22–23).

Solomon would probably have agreed with the old song "Sixteen Tons," made famous by Tennessee Ernie Ford, that said working brought only aging and more debt. In Solomon's case, the fruits of his labor brought not debt but despair. Those who work hard may never see the results of their labor. Their children may inherit the rewards without lifting a finger—and some even show their disrespect by squandering their parents' fortunes. Toil and trouble, foolishness and injustice, no respect and no remembrance: What's the use? Why not eat, drink, and be merry? Tomorrow we could all die anyway!

> The Lord didn't burden us with work; he blessed us with it.

Someone once said, "The thing most of us don't like about work is that it's so daily." We get up, go to work, come home, go to bed, get up, go to work, come home, go to bed, to start all over again. And in between we hear Solomon's voice saying, "What's it all about?"

That certainly isn't God's view of work. For six days God worked to create the earth and everything in it—including man. After each creation, God paused and said, "That's good!" He gave Adam a chance to share in his work: naming the animals and becoming a caretaker of the beautiful garden God created for him (Gen. 2:15, 19–20).

Some believe work is a good thing, that the Lord didn't burden us with work; he blessed us with it. How do you get from the daily *burden* of work to the daily *blessing* of work?

Some might reach that point at the end of the unemployment line, where the businessman in a three-hundred-dollar suit and the laborer in torn blue jeans find common ground. For others, like Tracy Woodall, the realization comes at the end of a longtime dream. When Tracy's husband and greatest encourager, Brent, died in the fateful September 11, 2001, attack on the World Trade Center, she may have wondered about the tension of burden versus blessing. Five weeks pregnant with her first child, Tracy grieved for nearly nine months. But when her daughter was born, so was a new dream.

In college Tracy had observed loving therapists transform a violent autistic girl into a loving child. Since then, she had always wanted to make a difference in the lives of autistic children. When she combined that misplaced longing and her commitment to keeping Brent's memory alive, she began to put together a nonprofit foundation in his name. A few years after the birth of her daughter, she birthed the Brent Woodall Foundation for Exceptional Children, as well as a foundation that helps autistic children in a Romanian orphanage. Tracy also adopted an orphaned baby girl from Russia.[28]

> When does work truly become a blessing? When we view our work as having eternal value.

I doubt that Tracy views life now as "meaningless, meaningless." Her work is indeed a blessing—to her and to others.

Sometimes the realization that work is a blessing comes at the end of our lives. So it seems with Solomon. In between the despair and the drudgery that seemed to characterize Solomon's life are these nuggets of truth: enjoying our work and the profits of it—be it minimum wage or maximum salary—are indeed gifts of God. And when we keep busy doing meaningful work, God will keep us so occupied with "gladness of heart" that we won't have time or energy to waste on regretting "the good ol' days" (see Eccles. 5:19-20).

Take a closer look at Solomon's words in Ecclesiastes 2:10-11 (italics mine): "all *my* work," "all *my* labor," "all that *my* hands had done," and "what *I* had toiled to achieve." No wonder Solomon's work seemed meaningless. King Solomon had denied himself nothing: women, wealth, pleasure—whatever his heart desired. He had built some magnificent buildings, including the tabernacle for God (1 Kings 8:13). But somewhere in the process, perhaps Solomon began thinking of that work as *his*.

Building monuments to ourselves will indeed result in meaningless work. When does work truly become a blessing? When we view our work as having eternal value. To his disciples, Jesus spoke these words: "Do not work for food that spoils, but for food that endures to eternal life, which the Son of Man will give you. On him God the Father has placed his seal of approval" (John 6:27).

How can you love what you do and know that it matters? When you do your work for God and to bless others—whether it's flipping pancakes or flying airplanes, building orphanages or broiling burgers—no matter how small or insignificant the task may seem, that work suddenly takes on new meaning. What's done for Christ is the work that will last.

That's when it all matters to God—and that's when it becomes a blessing for you.

PERSONAL TRUTH

When you work for God, everything matters.

PERSONAL PRAYER

Lord, when I'm tempted to see the work of my hands as the work of my hands, remind me that it is you who does any good work in me. You are my purpose; you are my reason for living. Thank you that your work always brings blessing and joy.

PERSONAL QUESTION

How do you view your work?

INTENTIONAL KINDNESS

I am the LORD, who exercises kindness,
justice and righteousness on earth,
for in these I delight.

—Jeremiah 9:24

The greatest thing a man can do for his Heavenly Father is to be kind to some of his other children."[29] Evidently a woman named Dorcas believed that statement long before Henry Drummond ever wrote it. Dorcas, obviously a woman of means, wanted to do more than just fill the pockets of the poor. She chose to get involved.

In the seacoast village of Joppa where Dorcas lived, the sea had claimed many husbands and fathers through storms and disasters. This kindhearted woman, a new Gentile believer, was filled with the joy and love only Christ could give. Few others in this family oriented society would place such an importance on doing kind acts for the poor.

But Dorcas was different, and the Jesus she loved compelled her to give more than just coins. Instead, Dorcas gave coats, undergarments—whatever clothing she could sew with her own hands. Each day she ascended to her upper room, laid out the materials, and began the nimble movement of loving fingers as they stitched piece by piece together.

Not only widows and orphans loved Dorcas. The Bible says she was "always doing good" (Acts 9:36). And her good works were a result of her faith, not a condition for earning God's favor.

But one day in the middle of sewing for the poor, Dorcas grew sick and died suddenly. Someone had heard that Peter was about twelve miles away, so they sent some men to find him. Dorcas was dead, but Peter and the disciples were doing miracles in the name of Jesus. Perhaps it was not too late.

> Her good works were a result of her faith, not a condition for earning God's favor.

By the time Peter arrived, Dorcas's body had been washed and prepared for burial and was lying in an upstairs room. As soon as Peter entered, a crowd of wailing widows lining the walls began to clutch their robes, which Dorcas had sewn. Eugenia Price imagined these probable words spoken by the widows to Peter: "Look at the rows of coats she has made—here are three half-finished. These bundles are all new undergarments made with her own hands for the poor who would otherwise live in rags. She not only clothed their bodies, Peter, she clothed their spirits with new hope."[30]

Peter, empowered by the Holy Spirit's indwelling, sent the crying women out of the room and prayed for the kind woman's healing. In a moment, Dorcas opened her eyes, smiled, and stood up. Peter presented her to the believers and widows, and the party began. Dorcas wasted no time. After hugging each woman and thanking God profusely, she probably picked up one of the unfinished garments and set to work enjoying the blessings God had given her.

Dorcas's influence reached beyond the widows and orphans of her community. Word about her life, her good works—and especially her resurrection—spread throughout Joppa. Many people believed in the Lord because of Dorcas's restoration (Acts 9:42). God obviously wasn't finished with her yet.

Have women like Dorcas disappeared? Are there any left in the twenty-first century? Two dozen senior women who call themselves The Henhouse Ministry have been busy showing kindness to the poor for over three decades. Some are stooped from age and arthritis; others wear hearing aids. These Southern widows, wives, mothers, and grandmothers represent a variety of vocations, churches, and rural communities. But they all share a common love and goal: their friendship, their faith, and the desire to give back because they have been so blessed themselves.

They meet every week to quilt, craft, and can vegetables and then work on projects alone as well. From those profits the women have given needy families food for Christmas, sponsored a student in Russia through seminary, and sent blankets to Romanian orphanages, winter coats to Armenia, Bibles and food to Russia, and various assistance to hospice families, flood victims, and widows.

When a West Virginia town's poverty reached an all-time high a few years ago, the Hens arrived with two trucks full of warm clothing and nonperishable food, fifty backpacks with school supplies, and Christmas stockings stuffed with toys, mittens, ponchos, and hats. In addition they served a spaghetti dinner to seventy-five residents.[31]

> Those who know that kindness is not a random act, but an intentional unwrapping of love, understand the Source of this great blessing.

Their ministry began when one elementary school principal was depressed about retiring. One day she saw a dump truck from a textile company pass by her school. She saw visions of quilts dancing in the fabric scraps of that truck—and she gathered her neighbors and friends together to form The Henhouse Ministry. The rest is history.[32]

Those who know that kindness is not a random act, but an intentional unwrapping of love, understand the Source of this great blessing: the King of kings, "The LORD . . . / sustains the fatherless and the widow" (Ps. 146:9). Those like Dorcas—and those unselfish Hens—must have experienced the God who exercises kindness (Isa. 63:7) Like the psalmist who asked, "How can I repay the LORD / for all his goodness to me?" they found a wonderful way to say, "Thank you!" (Ps. 116:12). Since we, too, are recipients of God's great blessing of goodness and kindness, can we do any less than be kind to his other children?

We don't have to be skilled in sewing, only skilled in loving. When we show kindness in the name of Jesus, we who are blessed already may become the very "scraps" God uses to rescue others from the dump trucks of life—the blessings that clothe others with the spirit of new joy, hope, and life.

PERSONAL TRUTH

Whatever you have is what God will use.

PERSONAL PRAYER

Father, when I had nothing, you gave me everything I needed. Thank you for showing kindness to me, even when I didn't even know you. Show me who needs my love and kindness today.

PERSONAL QUESTION

When was the last time someone blessed you with kindness?

SILVER CORDS AND GOLDEN BOWLS

They will still bear fruit in old age,
they will stay fresh and green,
proclaiming, "The LORD is upright;
he is my Rock, and there is no wickedness in him."

—Psalm 92:14–15

Perhaps you have asked the question, "How old is old?" On our twentieth birthdays, we think sixty is ancient. But the closer we get to fifty, we start the familiar denial process. "Why, he died so young! He was only sixty-five!"

Everyone has an opinion about old age. Some believe growing older is avoidable; they say, "To avoid old age, keep taking on new thoughts and throwing off old habits." Still others know it's inevitable: "Old age is the only thing that comes to us without effort." The bottom line? We all get there eventually.

The Bible puts a different slant on age. In the beginning, men seemed ageless, living for centuries, up to nine-hundred-plus years (Gen. 5). But after the Flood, man's years grew progressively shorter (Gen. 6:3). Abraham, the founder of the Hebrew nation, is one of the first men the Bible describes as elderly: "Abraham and Sarah were already old and well advanced in years, and Sarah was past the age of childbearing." Sarah questioned God and laughed when the Lord visited them and told her she would bear a child at age ninety. She considered Abraham "old" and herself "worn out" (Gen. 18:11–12).

But years don't matter to God. "Is anything too hard for the LORD? I will return to you at the appointed time next year and Sarah will have a son" (Gen. 18:14). Sarah lived until age 127; Abraham died at the "good old age" of 175—having received the son God promised (Gen. 23:1, 25:7).

God called some of his most faithful leaders into productive service in their senior years.

In the Jewish political and social system, people admired the aged and gave them a prominent place. Even in their private lives, the young were taught to respect their elders: "Rise in the presence of the aged, show respect for the elderly and revere your God" (Lev. 19:32). Their opinions were honored before others: "Now Elihu had waited before speaking to Job because they [Job's other friends] were older than he" (Job 32:4). And gray hair was not something you tried to cover up. It was a "crown of glory," indicating that a person's experience was a gift to be treasured and shared with others (Prov. 16:31 KJV). People also recognized it as a blessing God gave to those who knew him intimately and followed him with strong faith (Prov. 16:31).

God called some of his most faithful leaders into productive service in their senior years: Moses, Aaron, and Joshua were in their eighties; Caleb won his greatest battle at eighty-five; Anna, the eighty-four-year-old prophetess who recognized the infant Jesus as the promised Messiah, spent most of her widowed years fasting and praying in the temple. The Bible says that Moses died at the age of 120 in good health: "His eyes were not weak nor his strength gone" (Deut. 34:7).

What was these biblical giants' secret? More than anything, it was God's faithful promises: "Even in your old age and gray hairs

/ I am he, I am he who will sustain you. / I have made you and I will carry you; / I will sustain you and I will rescue you" (Isa. 46:4). The psalmist recognized this faithful trait of God throughout his life:

> *I was young and now I am old,*
> > *yet I have never seen the righteous forsaken*
> *or their children begging bread.*
> > *They are always generous and lend freely;*
> *their children will be blessed. (Psalm 37:25–26)*

But the psalmist also recognized the responsibility we have as well—to follow in a close relationship with God. His words echo the desires, no doubt, of every person:

> *The righteous will flourish like a palm tree . . .*
> > *planted in the house of the LORD,*
> *they will flourish in the courts of our God.*
> > *They will still bear fruit in old age,*
> *they will stay fresh and green. (Psalm 92:12–14)*

People are living longer today than a few decades back, but the reality is that all of us will not live to the "good old age" of eighty, ninety, or one hundred—because we live in a world where sickness and death steal good men and women early in life. But the psalmist pleaded with God to let him keep speaking about God's

> Knowing God—
> and making him
> known—is to be a
> lifelong passion.

faithfulness as long as he lived: "Even when I am old and gray, / do not forsake me, O God, / till I declare your power to the next generation, / your might to all who are to come" (Ps. 71:18).

The blessings of old age are numerous: the ability to see life through eyes of experience, to enjoy the fruit of our labors (and hopefully) numerous grandchildren, to savor the respect of many, and to grow in the wisdom to keep seeking after God's heart no matter how old we may be.

We have not earned the right, as some would counsel, to throw caution to the wind or to cease caring. King Solomon advised there is a time for all things—even rest—and a slowing down perhaps of our strength and energies. And he cautioned us to begin remembering, or honoring, our Creator while we are still young, before "the silver cord is severed, / or the golden bowl is broken"—when old age has crept in to diminish our senses (Eccl. 3:1-8, 12:6).

Perhaps the real blessing of old age comes when we can translate it into maturity, which, according to *Webster's*, means "full-grown, fully developed, or complete."[33] Abraham Lincoln said it well: "And in the end, it's not the years in your life that count. It's the life in your years."

Knowing God, and making him known, is to be a lifelong passion. Mature trees bear fruit as long as they have life. We, too, are given that privilege—and that blessing—to make every moment count, until our very breath is gone.

> *Shall we sit idly down and say,*
> *The night hath come; it is no longer day?*
> *The night hath not yet come; we are not quite*
> *Cut off from labor by the failing light;*
> *Something remains for us to do or dare;*
> *Even the oldest tree some fruit may bear.*
>   *—Henry Wadsworth Longfellow*

PERSONAL TRUTH

The old count with their fingers; the mature count with their lives.

PERSONAL PRAYER

Lord, just like the psalmist, we, too, pray for lives that will count for you. Teach us to number our days wisely, to live them passionately, and to serve you obediently—until our graves are sealed with the kiss of your approval.

PERSONAL QUESTION

How "old" are you?

Magic Words

One of them, when he saw he was healed,
came back, praising God in a loud voice.
He threw himself at Jesus' feet and thanked him—
and he was a Samaritan.

—Luke 17:15–16

Thanks! It's a powerful word. In the heart that longs for appreciation and acknowledgment, it can work magic. That one little word can paint a smile on a discouraged face and breathe life into a withered spirit. It can diffuse anger and incite joy.

Someone once said, "Gratitude is the most exquisite form of courtesy." A word of thanks can motivate us to keep on going, to continue the good work God has begun in us. Words of thanks— and even observing those with grateful hearts—will always bless the recipient.

Barbara Johnson tells the story of how one person's attitude of gratitude affected her. Her day started off rotten and progressively got worse: oversleeping, late to work, and major office stress. By the time she reached her bus stop to go home, her stomach was in knots. The bus was late and full, which meant she had to stand. She felt her depressive mood worsening with every bump and jolt of the bouncing bus.

But a voice from the front of the bus got her attention: "Beautiful day, isn't it?" She couldn't see the man, but she heard his cheery words all the way home as he commented on the beautiful scenery: This church. That park. A cemetery. The firehouse. His enthusiasm was contagious.

Barbara found herself smiling for the first time since her bad day had started. Just before she stepped off the bus, she finally caught a glimpse of the cheery man: "a plump figure with a black beard, wearing dark glasses, and carrying a thin white cane."[34]

> Words of thanks—and even observing those with grateful hearts—will always bless the recipient.

But what about the one who gives thanks—how is that person blessed? And what is the real power behind a spirit of gratitude?

One man found out. The other nine didn't stay around long enough to discover its secret. Jesus and his disciples were passing through a village somewhere between the border of Samaria and Galilee on the way to Jerusalem. Ten men huddled in a shady corner on the edge of town, obviously outcasts from the rest of the village. Word had traveled of this man Jesus, and of his power to heal the sick. Covered with the skin sores of dreaded leprosy, they dared not approach the Teacher and Healer.

The Jews treated leprosy as an extremely contagious disease and lepers as society's outcasts, doomed and shunned by everyone.[35] Furthermore, their isolation originated from God's direct command himself (Lev. 13:46; Num. 5:2–3). Still, standing from a safe distance, these lepers took a risk and yelled out to him, "Jesus, Master, have pity on us!" (Luke 17:13).

Jesus heard their cry and saw their pain. He told them to go and show themselves to the priest—inferring that they would be healed on the way. Examination by a priest was a Levitical law, and an action taken by anyone who had an infectious disease. The priest examined the victim and then determined whether that person was "clean" or "unclean" (see Lev. 13–14). So the men turned and ran to find a priest. On the way, they were indeed healed.

But in their mad sprint for freedom, one man suddenly stopped, perhaps looking at his arms and legs. He felt the new skin on his face, now as soft as that of a newborn baby. He changed directions, ran back to Jesus, realizing he could now touch the one who made him well. The man "threw himself at Jesus' feet and thanked him" (Luke 17:16).

Luke, the writer, added five qualifying words: "And he was a Samaritan." Jesus noted that fact as well. Perhaps talking to both the man and the other disciples and onlookers, Jesus added a question: "Were not all ten cleansed? Where are the other nine? Was no one found to return and give praise to God except this foreigner?" (Luke 17:17–18).

Scripture does not say, but Jesus seems to indicate that perhaps this is the only Samaritan of the ten (a "foreigner") and perhaps least likely to return, since Jews and Samaritans had no dealings with each other. Prejudice and hatred ran deep between the two races. Yet here one man threw away all his pride and honored the one who had just restored his health.

That's when the Samaritan leper found the real blessing of gratitude. The others were made physically well, but no one mentioned their faith or any healing of their spiritual condition. Jesus equated the grateful man's heart with personal acknowledgment of who he was—and a recognition that his healing had truly come from the Savior. To this man, Jesus offered total healing: "Rise and go; your faith has made you well" (Luke 17:19). A Greek word translated "well" here can also mean "saved" or "delivered," indicating a complete healing of the man's body, soul, and spirit.

> The blessing of gratitude is like a boomerang.

The blessing of gratitude is like a boomerang. When it flies out of a truly grateful heart, it hovers momentarily above the receiver, blessing its recipient, and then makes a 180-degree turn back into the life of the one who offered thanks.

Like a seed planted in fertile soil, it may spring up many kinds of flowered blessings. The Bible links a thankful heart to the additional blessing of peace. And not just any ordinary peace: when we offer our requests to God with a true spirit of thanksgiving, we are saying to God, "I trust into your safekeeping the answer to this prayer—and the solution to this dilemma. I give thanks to you because you are the Blessed Controller, and I have confidence you will do what is best for me."

When that happens, the Bible says, "the peace of God, which transcends all understanding, will guard your hearts and your minds in Christ Jesus" (Phil. 4:7). Needless to say, the Samaritan man who offered thanks to Jesus found not only complete healing, but the deep-down peace of God that's unexplainable by human minds.

The psalmist says repeatedly, "Give thanks to God." Jesus himself constantly offered praise to his heavenly Father for all things. And the apostle Paul's words remind us even further that giving thanks "is God's will for you in Christ Jesus" (1 Thess. 5:18).

The blessing of gratitude, of heartfelt thanks, always blesses the one who receives it. But it also can effect a spiritual change in the one with the attitude of gratitude. True thanks brings a smile to God's heart—and that's the best blessing of all.

PERSONAL TRUTH
Gratitude is the heart's best attitude.

PERSONAL PRAYER
Lord, how can I ever say "Thank you" enough for undeserved grace, unending mercies, unconditional love, and a thousand other blessings

you send daily? Help me to constantly demonstrate that same grateful attitude to others.

PERSONAL QUESTION

What are you most thankful for today?

DAY 22

Hurry Up and Wait

As [Moses] went over to look more closely,
he heard the Lord's voice: "I am the God of your fathers. . . .
Take off your sandals; the place where you are standing is holy
ground."

—Acts 7:30-33

What will you do?" "Are you sure about this?" "Why are
you leaving?"

The barrage of questions began the day my husband resigned a
pastorate—with no other prospects in view. He just felt it was
God's timing: that he had accomplished the things God put him
there to do.

Besides that, Larry had served as senior pastor for three years
following a long tenure as associate pastor. He felt God moving
him back into that associate pastor role. But normally, one
does not leave a position unless he has another waiting in the
wings.

The church generously gave us three weeks of vacation pay, as
well as five weeks of unused sabbatical, leaving us with eight weeks
to figure out the next step. So we waited, and we prayed. Throughout that eight-week "wilderness wandering," well-meaning friends
kept voicing their curiosity with even more questions: "Are you
moving away?" "Do you know where you'll go?"

"No, but God knows," I answered with a measure of confidence.

Then reaching to heaven for childlike reassurance, I prayed, "You do know what you're doing, don't you, Lord?"

Every morning we began the day by asking the Lord for direction. Every evening we went to bed with nothing new to report. The things we did check into remained closed doors.

> God has his own timetable—and his own reasons—for asking us to wait.

But God did know what he was doing. Our eight-week pay ended on a Friday. On Monday of the following week, Larry walked into his new office as associate pastor of another church, a thousand miles away. God took us away from longtime friends, but to us, the new place was holy ground. There were times during those weeks of waiting when we wondered what God was up to. But during that experience, God deepened our relationship with himself and with each other. It was the beginning of a faith relationship we have continued to pursue.

God has his own timetable—and his own reasons—for asking us to wait. At times, it may be a test of faith. If we refuse and rush in where only fools tread, we will suffer the consequences—as did King Saul.

After anointing Saul as king, the priestly prophet Samuel told Saul to wait seven days in Gilgal for his return. At that time, Samuel would offer the appropriate burnt offerings (1 Sam. 10:8). But on the seventh day, Saul panicked. Thousands of Philistines had surrounded the Israelites (1 Sam. 13:5). Many of Saul's men had gone AWOL and were hiding out in surrounding hills and caves. And Samuel was nowhere in sight.

Instead of waiting, Saul initiated a sacrificial burnt offering on his own—an act reserved for a Levite priest. About that time, Samuel showed up, and Saul paid for his disobedience with the eventual loss of his kingdom (see 1 Sam. 13:14). God will never allow man to steal his glory in an attempt to appease him or to save his own skin. We are never to substitute sacrifice for obedient waiting on the Lord. If we do, we will miss God's greater blessing.

Sometimes God allows periods of waiting to discipline us, but even in those moments, his plan is always to prepare us and to shape us for his use—as in the case of Moses. Pharaoh's daughter rescued and adopted him as a Hebrew baby, raising him as her own child in Egypt. Later as an adult, Moses decided to help God out and right a wrong, and it cost him forty years in the desert as a sheepherding tent dweller. Seeing one of his fellow Hebrew slaves being mistreated by an Egyptian, Moses intervened and killed the abuser—then hid him in the sand. The next day Moses tried to play God again, this time intervening in a fight between two Hebrew slaves. But the men had seen him kill the Egyptian, and the story spread until Pharaoh heard about it.

So Moses ran to escape his own death (Exod. 2:1-14). Forty years passed; forty years wasted. But maybe not. When Moses left so suddenly, I'm sure some of his Egyptian—and Hebrew—"family" wondered, *What will you do now, Moses? Where will you go?* Moses probably wondered too. But God used the time to prepare and toughen a leader who would one day deliver his people from years of slavery—and spend another forty years wandering in the wilderness—experiencing the blessings and miraculous power of an awesome God. It all started with a desert bush that wouldn't stop burning.

"God is more interested in a love relationship with you than He is in what you can do for Him."

It was there that Moses met God for the first time. And the moment was such a holy one, God told Moses to remove his dirty sandals. Moses would soon learn that *anywhere* God is, is holy ground. God continued to shape Moses all of his life, but Moses' time of waiting had served its purpose. God was interested in building a relationship with Moses and the people he had chosen.

If you find yourself in a waiting situation someday—and we all will—whether it is raising toddlers or teenagers, making sense of a job termination, handling a chronic or terminal illness, or hoping for an end to singleness, Henry Blackaby's words may help:

> *If you do not have clear instructions from God in a matter, pray and wait. Learn patience. Depend on God's timing. His timing is always right and best. Don't get in a hurry. He may be withholding directions to cause you to seek Him more intently. Don't try to skip over the relationship to get on with* doing. *God is more interested in a love relationship with you than He is in what you can do for Him.*[36]

When we trust God's timing, he gets the glory. Waiting on God may not seem like a blessing, but behind the scenes God is working out his perfect will, in his perfect way. It's fairly easy to spot those who have experienced that blessing.

You can smell the fragrance of God all over them.

PERSONAL TRUTH

It's good to wait on God. But it's even better to wait with *God.*

PERSONAL PRAYER

Lord, when impatience threatens, remind me that you have never forgotten me. Teach me the lessons I need to learn during those times when nothing is happening. Have your own way, Lord, not mine!

PERSONAL QUESTION

In what situation is it most difficult for you to wait on God?

DAY 23

True Disciples or
Reluctant Followers?

*Jesus replied, "No one who has left home or brothers or sisters
or mother or father or children or fields for me and the gospel
will fail to receive a hundred times as much in this present age
(homes, brothers, sisters, mothers, children and fields—
and with them, persecutions) and in the age to come, eternal life."*

—Mark 10:29–30

His boat was missing; where had he gone? Only yesterday
he had filled their stomachs with miraculous food! Had
they dreamed it? Surely he would be their long-awaited king. But
it didn't take long for the eager crowd to discover that Jesus and
his disciples had rowed across the lake to Capernaum. So off the
crowd went to find him.

Jesus recognized the intent of these sensational seekers immediately.

*You've come looking for me not because you saw God in my actions
but because I fed you, filled your stomachs—and for free. Don't waste
your energy striving for perishable food like that. Work for the food
that sticks with you, food that nourishes your lasting life, food the Son
of Man provides. He and what he does are guaranteed by God the
Father to last. (John 6:26–27 MSG)*

Jesus explained his words, but the people couldn't accept them. They wanted temporary gain; Jesus was teaching eternal truths and values. The Bible says, "From this time many of his disciples turned back and no longer followed him" (John 6:66). I'm sure many "followers" watched from afar, but none chose to heed his teachings as true disciples.

> Discipleship may lead us to poverty or wealth, to fame or anonymity; but it will be God's individual call to us.

Jesus then turned his attention to his own twelve disciples. "You do not want to leave too, do you?" (John 6:67). Jesus already knew one of them would betray him permanently in the end—and that the rest of the twelve would scatter temporarily at his death.

But Peter, self-appointed spokesman for the dozen, made a bold and honorable statement: "Lord, to whom shall we go? You have the words of eternal life. We believe and know that you are the Holy One of God" (John 6:68–69). Even Peter himself would follow only "at a safe distance" later at the time of Jesus' arrest (Luke 22:54 MSG).

Jesus spent endless hours and energy teaching his disciples the difference between true disciples and reluctant followers. What is true discipleship? Does it spell life—or death? How do you discern a true *disciple* from merely a distant *follower*?

A German theologian named Dietrich Bonhoeffer believed that "when Christ calls a man, he bids him come and die."[37] He said to find out what the call to discipleship meant, we would have to ask Jesus himself.

Jesus reminds us we are not above our Teacher (Matt. 10:24). He asks nothing less than a total denial of our own desires, in an exchange for his (Luke 14:33). Bonhoeffer, who was executed in a German prison for his faith, says, "It is not for us to choose which way we will follow. That depends on the will of Christ."[38] Discipleship may lead us to poverty or wealth, to fame or anonymity;

but it will be God's individual call to us. And God usually chooses to test our faith at the root of our heart desires.

Bonhoeffer demonstrated well that discipleship is not something we tack on to Christianity—it *is* Christianity. God wants our highest affection. He may not require us to give up everything we love, but he wants us to be willing. Above all, discipleship requires that we die to our own selfish desires, our own self-will, and our own temptations for self-control.

Perhaps that's truly the difference between followers and disciples. *Followers* want to place one foot in their shallow faith, and one foot in their selfish desires. At the slightest hint of trouble, they turn back.

True *disciples,* however, place both feet in the grave from a death to self but still stand on the solid ground of devotion to the one who leads them—no matter what the cost or where the journey ends. Peter and the other ten disciples all fled at the first sign of adversity, yet each finished well after the Holy Spirit empowered them to go and make disciples of all nations. It's not how we start, but how we finish, that counts.

Chris Tiegreen says,

> *The cost of* not *following Jesus is even greater than the cost of discipleship. Those who do not follow Him—even those who follow Him, but not wholeheartedly—miss all of the blessings and benefits of being completely sold out to Christ. They miss intimate fellowship with the Creator of all that is; they miss the power of God at work in their lives; they miss the peace and fullness of knowing they are right with God. And they will miss great eternal rewards.*[39]

How is discipleship a blessing? Jesus said no one who has left all for him—family, home, land—would fail to receive "a hundred times as much in this present age . . . and in the age to come, eternal life" (Mark 10:30). That's a ten-thousand-times return on our investments! William MacDonald interprets these dividends in a way consistent with Jesus' teaching. After all, Jesus speaks freely about how a life of ease and riches too easily chokes out our devotion to him.

> Discipleship is not something we tack on to Christianity—it *is* Christianity.

MacDonald views these blessings as new family members in God's kingdom: hospitality in more homes as a servant of the Lord, open doors to the gospel in other lands, and yes, actual persecutions—which Jesus considers as cause of rejoicing when suffering for his sake—and a greater capacity to enjoy eternity in heaven.[40]

Perhaps Thomas à Kempis explained this blessing clearly: "Blessed is he that knoweth how good it is to love Jesus, and for His sake to despise himself. . . . Love Him, therefore, and hold Him thy friend; for when all others forsake thee, He will not forsake thee, nor suffer thee finally to perish."[41]

The best blessing of discipleship is believing—and knowing—that the one for whom we are willing to forsake all will never forsake us. That makes it all worthwhile.

PERSONAL TRUTH

Followers find reasons to watch from afar. Disciples come eagerly, just as they are.

PERSONAL PRAYER

Lord, indeed, where would we go if not to you? Strengthen weary legs and arms that we might follow you wherever you go, embracing others with your love and compassion along the way. Help us sense your heartbeat in the works that really matter. Knowing you makes any sacrifice worth it all.

PERSONAL QUESTION

How has discipleship been a blessing on your journey so far?

VANISHED!

Enoch walked steadily with God.
And then one day he was simply gone:
God took him.

—Genesis 5:24 MSG

Webster's Dictionary defines integrity as the "state of being complete," an "unbroken condition," "wholeness," or "uprightness."[42] Sometimes pride gets in the way of integrity and causes a break in that "state of being complete." A friend of ours understood and experienced the blessings of integrity, but only after a test of his pride.

Chet is one of the kindest, godliest men we know. But he is human. It seems he was poking around at a garage sale when he spied an electric saw at a bargain price. Pleased with his find, he headed home to try it out. To his chagrin, when he plugged it in, it only buzzed. Back to the garage sale he went, only to discover that the previous owner of the saw would not return his money. Chet was more than a little hot under the collar. As the man started explaining his rationale for not refunding the purchase price, in mid-sentence Chet spun around in anger and strode back to his vehicle.

He got in his truck and had started down the road when his wife, Millie, who had come along for moral support, leaned over and said, "Are you going back now or later?" Convicted to the quick over his rash behavior, Chet wheeled the truck around and headed back to the man's house. As he knocked, the man slowly and cautiously came to the door, not knowing what to expect from this irate customer.

"Sir," Chet began, "I am a Christian, and I came back to ask your forgiveness for my rude behavior a few minutes ago. Could you find it in your heart to forgive me?" With that, the man instantly reached into his pocket and produced the eight dollars in question. He said, "Here's your money back. I should have been more careful about putting out a saw when I wasn't sure how well it worked."

Sometimes pride gets in the way of integrity.

"Thank you," Chet responded, "but I no longer want the money. My only need is your forgiveness. Will you forgive me?"

"Yeah, sure. I forgive you."

Another man experienced the blessings of integrity in a most unusual way. Enoch was the great-great-great grandson of Seth, the son of Adam, starting a generation of men who "began to call on the name of the LORD" (Gen. 4:26). He was the father of the oldest man who ever lived, Methuselah, who died at the ripe old age of 969.

Perhaps there was something about being a father that brought him face-to-face with what was really important in life. Maybe it was Enoch's godly heritage. For whatever reason, the Bible says after the birth of Methuselah, Enoch walked with God three hundred years. Or maybe it simply means Enoch lived "*another* three hundred years in fellowship with God," as *The Living Bible* paraphrases it (TLB, italics mine). Regardless, that's a long time to walk with God. And you don't learn to walk with God in a day. The idea is a continual, unbroken condition, wholeness, a state of being upright with God. *Hmm.* Sort of like integrity.

But then the Bible says Enoch vanished. God took him. What a way to go! Lest you think that means death, the New Testament explains further: "By faith Enoch was taken from this life, so that he did not experience death; he could not be found, because God had taken him away" (Heb. 11:5).

Can you imagine the scene? His son Methuselah and other sons and daughters came home for a visit. Where's Dad? Not in the living room. He wasn't taking a shower. No one in the backyard. No dirty dishes in the kitchen; he hadn't eaten supper yet. Where was he? And then they spied his long robe crumpled on the floor and his sandals right beside it. About that time Enoch's wife walked in from next door, teary-eyed, with a mysterious explanation. She was talking to him, and Enoch had just—disappeared.

To figure out why God chose to do such a thing would require being God, and we are not God. Elijah the prophet is the only other mortal man we know God "translated" or escorted to heaven without physical death (2 Kings 2:11–12).

No one ever lived who was perfect, except Jesus Christ, the Son of God. Yet somewhere in Enoch's life, he latched on to a promise God gave him, and Enoch believed God. While Enoch still walked with God on earth, the Bible says "he was commended as one who pleased God. And without faith," it adds, "it is impossible to please God. . . . Anyone who comes to him must believe that he exists and that he rewards [blesses] those who earnestly seek him" (Heb. 11:5–6).

> The sweetest blessing of that steady walk of integrity is the fellowship we have with God.

"Blessed are they," says the psalmist, "whose ways are blameless," who "seek him with all their heart. . . . / They walk in his ways" (Ps. 119:1–3). Enoch was a man of faith, a man who earnestly sought God, one who knew him personally.

Enoch was a man of integrity. He received an enviable reward: nonstop, uninterrupted fellowship with his Maker. Who wouldn't want to beam up to heaven and escape the painful throes of death?

But unless Jesus comes again before our death, we will indeed all die a physical death. The good news is, walking with God is a choice and reality we can all experience now. The sweetest blessing of that steady walk of integrity is the fellowship we have with God.

Because of our relationship with Jesus, it's a fellowship that only we can break. The relationship between Parent and child never changes. His forgiveness is past, present, and future. But the moment we, like Chet, realize the link of fellowship has been broken through pride or disobedience, and we humble ourselves before him, we will once again be walking steadily with God.

One day a heavenly trumpet will sound. Christ will descend from heaven, and every man, woman, and child who ever walked with God by faith will be transported into God's presence. Vanished! Nonstop, uninterrupted, eternal fellowship.

How can we be sure? Because integrity is one of God's best attributes—and one of his best blessings.

PERSONAL TRUTH

An elaborate cover on a cheap book is useless.

PERSONAL PRAYER

Lord, teach me to walk in your integrity, knowing that the reward and blessing include daily, uninterrupted fellowship with you. May my walk, though imperfect, be characterized by the sweet savor of heaven.

PERSONAL QUESTION

What areas of integrity challenge you the most?

LITTLE HEAD, BIG HEART

Know-it-alls don't like being told what to do;
*   they avoid the company of wise men and women. . . .*
An intelligent person is always eager to take in more truth.

—Proverbs 15:12, 14 MSG

H ave you ever known someone whose head was bigger than his heart? Al Bryant relates what happened to one young, gifted pastor

whose preaching was a cut above the ordinary. As the ranks of his congregation began to swell, his head followed suit. After he had delivered his latest barnburner one morning, one of his loyal parishioners earnestly shook his hand and said, "You're becoming one of the greatest expositors of this generation, pastor."

As he squeezed his head into the car and slid behind the steering wheel, his weary wife alongside him and all the kids stuffed into the back seat, he could not resist sharing the story.

"Mrs. Franklin told me she thought I was one of the greatest expositors of this generation," he said proudly, caught up in the heady swirl of the woman's exaggerated compliment.

No response.

Fishing for affirmation, he glanced at his silent wife with a weak smile and prodded, "I wonder just how many 'great expositors' there are in this generation?"

Unable to resist the opportunity to set the record straight, she said quietly, "One less than you think, my dear."[43]

In the first century, an eloquent preacher by the name of Apollos could have gotten a big head too. A Jew by birth from Egypt, Apollos knew the Old Testament well.

> "I did this because I wanted your faith to stand firmly upon God, not on man's great ideas."

Like Paul, Apollos preached with power, and his zealous, enthusiastic spirit attracted many followers. He knew John the Baptist's message by heart and, though Jesus had come, died, and been resurrected, he was still challenging people to repent and prepare for the coming Messiah (Acts 18:24-28).

But in at least two ways, Apollos and Paul differed. One was in their preaching styles. Apollos was known for his charismatic personality and stunning sermons. As his ministry progressed, he was so dynamic that the Christians in Corinth actually formed two camps: those who followed Paul and those who followed Apollos. The people had elevated the man to equal the message. Anytime that happens, trouble soon follows.

Paul, whose name means "little," claimed no such eloquence. In fact, he made clear his purpose was never to impress. And apparently committees were not beating down Paul's doors to enlist him for their next motivational speaker. From Paul's own mouth to the Corinthians came these words:

When I first came to you I didn't use lofty words and brilliant ideas to tell you God's message. . . . I came to you in weakness—timid and trembling. And my preaching was very plain, not with a lot of oratory and human wisdom, but the Holy Spirit's power was in my words, proving to those who heard them that the message was from God. I did

*this because I wanted your faith to stand firmly upon God, not on
man's great ideas. (1 Corinthians 2:1, 3–5 TLB)*

When jealousy and quarreling erupted: "Our preacher is better
than your preacher!" Paul set them straight. Both of them were
simply servants, vessels God used so people would come to know
Christ. Paul was the planter—the one who first came, sowing the
seed. But Apollos added water—and both are important in God's
work. But the key ingredient in growth, Paul added, is God—who
makes all things grow (1 Cor. 3:6–9).

At least Paul and Apollos agreed on the same message. But it
wasn't always that way. Paul, addressing the Corinthians, determined to "speak only of Jesus Christ and his death on the cross"
(1 Cor. 2:2 TLB). Where did Apollos stand on this issue? And how
did he respond to all the flattery of being equated with Paul's ministry? Did he swell up like the pastor who was praised for his great
expository skills? Did he claim to be superior? The fact that Apollos said nothing may testify to his teachable spirit.

Early in Apollos's ministry, his message differed from Paul's. Apollos knew the Old Testament story—but he was clueless about the real
good news. Jesus had come! Jesus was the Messiah. John the Baptist had done his preparatory
work. But Jesus finished the Father's work.

Aquila and Priscilla, friends and fellow tent-
makers with Paul, heard Apollos when he was
just a young upstart of a preacher in the town
of Ephesus years earlier. Fiery yet smooth.
Eager, bold, impassioned—and eloquent indeed. This gentle couple invited Apollos to their home and told him the rest of the
story. They could have gruffly corrected him and bruised his
spirit. And Apollos could have argued with them, rejecting their

> Because of
> Apollos's
> response, the
> blessing of a
> teachable spirit
> brought God into
> action.

helpful criticism with an "I know what I'm talking about—don't try to teach me" attitude. But in a spirit of maturity, both responded well. And because of Apollos's response, the blessing of a teachable spirit brought God into action (Acts 18:26–28).

Others saw Apollos's genuine heart and began to encourage him, sending letters of commendation to the other disciples. The Bible says Apollos was a "great help to those who by grace had believed" (Acts 18:27). And God gave him even greater boldness, believability, and power.

It's no wonder crowds mistakenly tried to put Apollos on a pedestal with Paul. But evidently he had no trouble squeezing his head through the door of his home or his church. When God blesses with a teachable spirit, he shrinks the head but enlarges the heart.

PERSONAL TRUTH

If your hat is too small, check your heart size before you buy a bigger hat.

PERSONAL PRAYER

Lord, I don't need more knowledge, eloquence, or opportunity. If my message does not include you, I have no message. May my heart always be receptive to your Spirit's leading and teaching.

PERSONAL QUESTION

How do you respond to criticism?

A-Count-Ability

Let me fall into the hands of the LORD,
for his mercy is very great;
but do not let me fall into the hands of men.

—1 Chronicles 21:13

The current U.S. defense budget is one of the largest in American history. We live in an age where terrorism and danger stalk us daily. Who doesn't want a strong defense? Who doesn't want to be protected from outside forces against the very freedom we have fought for so dearly through the years? Someone once said, "The United States is determined that there shall be no more wars and is equally determined to be ready for the next one."

At one time in his life, a king named David probably agreed with that statement. Perhaps his thoughts were something like these: *A huge fighting army is necessary. We have been successful in battle all these years. Hmmmm. I wonder how many fighting men are really in my kingdom. How many do we need? How big is our army? Do we need more? Exactly how secure are we? Well, there's only one way to find out.*

In 1 Chronicles 21 we read that David insisted on taking a census with instructions to list every fighting man even though Joab, his commander, tried to persuade him to change his mind. Not only was David's decision repulsive to Joab, it also angered God

(v. 6). Why? Apparently David was relying upon the strength of his army, not in the strength of God.

The numbering took almost ten months to complete (2 Sam. 24:8). Before anyone else confronted him about his sin in taking the census, David came to his own senses and admitted his foolishness and his great sin to God. But his actions had infuriated God, and God gave David a multiple choice: "Do you want the punishment behind door number one, door number two, or door number three?" God would forgive, but he required one of these as payment: "three years of famine, three months of being swept away before your enemies, with their swords overtaking you, or three days of the sword of the LORD—days of plague in the land, with the angel of the LORD ravaging every part of Israel" (1 Chron. 21:12).

> Those who follow God's leading and counsel will bring not destruction, but blessing to a nation.

David was like a broken, repentant child. He had experienced the wrath and the mercy of God. Perhaps his thoughts flashed back to all the times God had rescued him, and to all the beautiful songs he composed on his harp: "I will praise you, O LORD. . . . / For great is your love, higher than the heavens; / your faithfulness reaches to the skies" (Ps. 108:3-4). David said, "I am in deep distress. Let me fall into the hands of the LORD, for his mercy is very great; but do not let me fall into the hands of men" (1 Chron. 21:13).

The foolish decisions of leaders have claimed countless numbers of lives. War is sometimes both necessary and unavoidable, but if we rely on ourselves and not God, the results will be disastrous. Those who follow God's leading and counsel will bring not destruction, but blessing to a nation.

After a plague killed seventy thousand men, an angel prepared to destroy Jerusalem. God allowed David to see the angel who was standing "between heaven and earth, with a drawn sword in his hand extended over Jerusalem" (1 Chron. 21:16). David pleaded for the lives of his people, and God instructed him to go build an altar on what was the threshing floor of a Gentile named Araunah.

Araunah cheerfully offered to give the materials for the burnt offering: oxen, wood, wheat, whatever was necessary, for free. But David realized that a sacrifice must cost something. Seventy thousand men had died, and David was willing to pay a high price to build his altar to God. As soon as David offered the payment, God told the angel that the destruction was over (1 Chron. 21:27). The site of that sacrifice was the same place David chose as a permanent house for God—the famous Solomon's temple (2 Chron. 3:1).

For us, Jesus Christ became the lasting sacrifice, the permanent atonement, the perfect offering that insures his blessing to those who trust in him, not themselves.

In taking the census, David's pride must have caused him to forget temporarily the rest of that psalm he wrote to God: "Give us aid against the enemy, / for the help of man is worthless. / With God we will gain the victory, / and he will trample down our enemies" (Ps. 108:12–13).

> Jesus Christ became the lasting sacrifice, the permanent atonement, the perfect offering that insures his blessing to those who trust in him, not in themselves.

The best of man's defenses are useless unless God is on his side. "Blessed is the nation whose God is the LORD" (Ps. 33:12). Pity the people who forget that truth—and do not understand the magnitude of that blessing. God help the nation that prides itself in human strength yet ignores the one who is its Strength.

But enjoy, give thanks, and count your blessings if you live in a nation that chooses to place its life and future in the hands of the one true, merciful God.

Personal Truth

Blessed is the nation who counts its blessings from God daily.

Personal Prayer

Lord, keep our nation strong, with eyes always fixed on you, so that we might inherit the blessing of a godly nation. Bless our leaders with the wisdom that comes only from you. Help me to encourage and pray for them daily. Without you, we are without hope.

Personal Question

How can you pray for your nation and its leaders today?

DAY 27

GOD IS BIGGER THAN WE THINK

"You do not know me or my Father," Jesus replied.
"If you knew me, you would know my Father also."

—John 8:19

To some people," says Dan Bennett, "God is a peg to hang their troubles on." Albert Einstein called God a "scientist." Elizabeth Barrett Browning thought of him as a "poet," and Martin Luther referred to God as "A mighty fortress." Some refer to God as a "higher power," but poet John Greenleaf Whittier joins a host of others who believe he is "a God of love."

Do all those people know who God really is? Or more importantly, do they really know God? If you read my book *40 Days in God's Presence*, I hope you came to know God in a greater way as we tried to learn of his character through the eyes of those who knew him personally. But even those who encountered God in the Bible struggled at times with how to describe him:

Jonah: A determined, merciful Pursuer
Daniel: A Lion Tamer and a faithful Deliverer
Ruth: My Redeemer and a Defender of widows
Noah: A Shelter from the storm
Isaiah: A holy and exalted God
The Prodigal Son: A forgiving Father
Abraham: God, the Provider and Promise Keeper

The Children of Israel: A Jealous God
Lot: One to be feared
David: My Shepherd

> **Many tend to define God based more on their experience, teaching, gifts, and even their upbringing.**

Many tend to define God based on their experience, teaching, gifts, and even their upbringing. Years ago, I attended a seminar that included what I'll call *family structuring*. In this exercise, one volunteer selected several willing participants to represent his/her family members. The key volunteer played him- or herself. The one structuring his family placed the members wherever he desired in the room and whispered to them what they should do or what facial expressions they should wear. Then he placed himself anywhere he wanted within the family structure. After everyone was in place, the seminar leader said, "Freeze." And several seconds passed while we made our own observations of each "family member."

The results of these experiments were quite revealing. One in particular placed the head of his home standing on a chair, arms curved and fingers stretched out like an eagle's talons ready to attack the bird's prey. There, the "father" hovered powerfully over the other family members—and all of them, even though they were only actors, felt the impact of that moment. So did the one who had created the scene for his family as he looked up at the one standing over him.

During those "structured" moments, we caught a glimpse of how our families often function—or dysfunction—at least according to our own perspectives. But a wise leader also showed us how our own families sometimes shape our image of God, especially from the way we perceive our earthly fathers. Wrong or incomplete images can result in an imbalance. God is righteous, but he is not an overpowering ogre. He is loving, but he also disciplines.

If we are not careful, we will try to bring God down to our level of understanding and create a God that is much too small. If we can explain every facet of God's workings, then perhaps our knowledge and experience are too limited. God is too big to define, yet he can be known intimately and personally. How?

Some people in the Bible thought they knew God, and that their images of him were superior. In reality, they didn't have a clue. For example, one day, the Jewish Pharisees were challenging Jesus as he taught in the temple. For a truth to be acceptable, law required two or three witnesses to verify that truth. Yet there was Jesus, whom they saw as just another man; Jesus, son of a carpenter, claiming to be the truth and light. His witnesses? He testified for himself, and his other witness was his Father. When the Pharisees, whose image of God was as a giver and keeper of laws, questioned Jesus as to who his father was, Jesus replied, "If you knew me, you would know my Father also" (John 8:19).

Later in Jerusalem the Jewish leaders again questioned who he was. This time, Jesus spoke even more plainly: "I and the Father are one" (John 10:30). Incensed, they tried to stone Jesus, not because of something he did, such as performing miracles, but because of who he was: Jesus, the Son of God. And because Jesus claimed to be God himself.

> God is too big to define, yet he can be known intimately and personally.

Jesus said, "If you knew me, you would know my Father also." Do you want to know God? Then you must personally encounter Jesus. Do you want to know what God is like? Look at his Son. The Bible says Jesus is the "image of the invisible God, the firstborn over all creation" (Col. 1:15).

Watch Jesus as he cradles little children in his arms, and you'll see the tenderness of God. See Jesus stoop down to encourage a broken woman, and observe God's compassion. Listen to his parable of the prodigal son and discover God's forgiveness. Watch him overturn the money changers' tables in the temple, and witness God's righteous anger. And look at Jesus as he is being crucified with arms outstretched for you, and see God's love.

God is just, and he is holy. He is the Resurrection, and he is Life. He is the Judge and the Redeemer, the Author and Finisher of our faith. He is the Highest Power, because he is the only Power. He is jealous, because he is Love itself.

Man's loftiest words still can't come close to explaining or describing God. He is infinite and indefinable, yet he chose to make a way for our finite minds to grasp knowing him. Seeing God through Jesus' eyes keeps us from trying to squeeze God into our own molds of experience or incomplete understanding. And it always results in balance—not in the sense of "making God big," as A. W. Tozer says, because "you cannot make God bigger." Instead, he says, "we are only to see Him bigger"—like a star through a telescope.[44]

No matter what our experiences, our upbringing, or what others tell us, when we admit our inadequacy in defining such a great God and instead see him through the person of Jesus, that's when the real blessing comes.

In reality, we can experience the blessing of knowing God intimately only by knowing Jesus intimately—because when you see Jesus, you've seen God. He and the Father are one.

PERSONAL TRUTH

Those who see God only through their eyes have already reduced him to their size.

PERSONAL PRAYER

God, you are bigger than I can imagine, feel, or comprehend. That you made a way through Jesus for me to know you personally makes me feel so small and unworthy. Enlarge my heart and my vision so I can embrace your fullness. I am so thirsty for you, God!

PERSONAL QUESTION

How big is your God?

The Secret Game of Life

As long as he sought the LORD,
God gave him success.

—2 Chronicles 26:5

Is success really a blessing or a curse? Perhaps it all depends on your definition of success. Everyone has one. Many people believe wholeheartedly in one of *Webster's* definitions: "the gaining of wealth, fame, rank."[45]

Some will argue that you must have a dream—a magnificent obsession—a desire strong enough to drive you to success. After all, true success is the ability to reach your dreams. Another says connection is at the heart of success: the sum total of the people with whom you communicate and connect. Great motivators like John Maxwell write books to tell us we must change our thinking patterns if we ever want to reach a measure of success.

Depending on whom you talk to, you can find there are seven, eight, eleven, and up to a hundred secrets to success—each one swearing his or her formula holds the key. But who's right? And what on earth *is* success?

Some well-known sports figures apparently experienced success. They acquired fame, multimillion-dollar contracts, and the perks associated with them. But their status often resulted in heady power and pride, and "success" turned into a curse.

But others, like Joe Gibbs, Hall of Fame NFL coach, tell a different story. When Gibbs was asked how he got the job as head coach of the Washington Redskins, he enjoyed replying, "I have no earthly idea! Just strictly through God's blessing, I guess."[46] Joe did have a dream—of coaching in the NFL one day. Seventeen years after starting out, he realized that dream as head coach of the Redskins.

> "Establishing a personal relationship with Christ is so important, because it affects every other decision you make in life."

But Joe Gibbs will tell you that a turning point in his life in 1972 crystallized the meaning of success for him, and he certainly changed his thinking patterns. He turned to Christ at the age of nine, but Joe moved away from God in his teen and college years. As he began to communicate and connect with more people in his career whose lives God had touched miraculously, he realized what he needed to do. Gibbs made the most important connection of all: "Establishing a personal relationship with Christ is so important, because it affects every other decision you make in life," he says.[47]

Joe notes, "We're playing in the game of life, and God is our head coach. But if we're not studying the game plan [God's Word], that's like the Washington Redskins not studying their game plan. And that's crazy!"[48]

Henry David Thoreau wrote, "Why should we be in such desperate haste to succeed, and in such desperate enterprises? If a man does not keep pace with his companions, perhaps it is because he hears a different drummer." Perhaps Gibbs would be the first to agree.

So would a teenager named Uzziah—until he stopped listening to the right Drummer and let success go to his head. The people of Judah crowned Uzziah king when he was only sixteen years old. The Bible says he ruled for fifty-two years and did what was right in God's eyes, just like his father, Amaziah. We read, "As long as he sought the LORD, God gave him success" (2 Chron. 26:5). It was God who *gave* him success—meaning he prospered and thrived as a great and wise king.

Uzziah stacked up an impressive list of accomplishments during his reign: With God's help he defeated enemies, built towers, and rebuilt towns. He dug cisterns, developed a well-trained army, and amassed great weapons of defense. The Bible says Uzziah's "fame spread far and wide, for he was greatly helped until he became powerful" (2 Chron. 26:15).

But it was at that point that Uzziah's success suddenly plummeted. He decided to try something God had reserved only for priests: in a spirit of pride, he entered the temple to burn incense on the altar, a task strictly reserved for priests. Eighty-one priests actually followed Uzziah into the temple and confronted him. Uzziah's discipline was swift and definitive: God struck him with leprosy. Uzziah lived the rest of his life isolated from the palace *and* the temple (2 Chron. 26:16–21).

In God's eyes, success has nothing to do with superficial wealth, fame, or rank—though he may decide to bless that way. A very wise God blesses us with his personalized success when we seek him and follow his secret game plan for life. And that plan will alter our thinking patterns:

> In God's eyes, success has nothing to do with superficial wealth, fame, or rank—though he may decide to bless that way.

Be careful to obey all the law my servant Moses gave you; do not turn from it to the right or to the left, that you may be successful wherever you go. Do not let this Book of the Law depart from your mouth; meditate on it day and night, so that you may be careful to do everything written in it. Then you will be prosperous and successful. (Joshua 1:7–8)

Listening to the right Drummer will bring us into God's Hall of Fame, and into his blessings. The Law—God's Word—tells us what the secrets are. But it is that secure relationship with the Lord Jesus Christ that blesses us with the power to obey—and to enjoy his definition of success.

PERSONAL TRUTH

Success is when you agree with God on what is most important.

PERSONAL PRAYER

Lord, help me to follow your game plan for success. Let the words of your heart penetrate my own until I am completely saturated with you.

PERSONAL QUESTION

Where have you looked for success?

CANCELED!

Then Jesus said to her,
"Your sins are forgiven. . . .
Your faith has saved you; go in peace."

—Luke 7:48, 50

It takes courage to admit weakness or sin. Most of us would rather hide it in the darkness than expose it to the light.

A staff member at a large church "hid" for years. As a young university student he had tried marijuana and other drugs but gave them up after he graduated. A few years later, however, he was involved in a car accident causing extensive injuries. Major surgery followed, requiring large doses of medication to stop the pain. The experience brought back memories of his college days with marijuana.

When he left the hospital, he couldn't quell the insatiable desire for drugs. Tears welled up, and his fists clenched when he admitted how for years he had lied to his wife about working late at the office. All those hours he spent secretly driving up and down back alleys of a nearby city, making deals for drugs he so desperately wanted.

Then one day, his wife found out. Out of respect for her husband, she kept his secret but pleaded with him to get help. He couldn't stop himself.

Drugs were ruining his health, his marriage, and his future. He had come to the conference as a last resort. The following week he was going to resign from his position at the church. How could he ever repay his family and church for the time he had stolen from them? He was extremely depressed and contemplated suicide.

But as he finished unloading his pain, for the first time that week his countenance changed. And as one by one, each conferee surrounded him with tears of empathy, comfort, and acceptance, he felt relief. "I should have done this a long time ago. But I was so ashamed, so proud, so scared," he confessed. "I cannot do this myself. I will need help." Admitting the truth filled him with new hope and gave him light for his dark tunnel.

Sin turns our lives into churning volcanoes—places of turmoil, void of lasting peace. Someone else, a woman, tired of her darkness and shame, dared to embrace the light. And it changed her life forever.

She is described simply as "a woman who had lived a sinful life" (Luke 7:37). Was she a harlot, an unfaithful wife, an unscrupulous businesswoman, or a malicious gossip? Most believe her sins probably involved sexual misconduct, but is it really important? It wasn't to Jesus.

Others, however, felt differently. Jesus had been invited to a Pharisee's home for dinner. But this uninvited guest showed up, bringing an extravagant gift for Jesus. The "sinful" woman dropped at Jesus' feet, and began to wash Jesus' dusty feet with her tears, as she wept uncontrollably. She draped her long locks of hair over his feet to dry them, kissed them, then took her precious gift of alabaster perfume—perhaps the only thing of value she owned—and poured it over Jesus' feet.

The woman's actions angered the host, Simon, a Pharisee: *What is she doing? And what is Jesus thinking? He should not tolerate a woman's touching him, much less a sinful woman like her! If he really is a prophet, he would know what she is!*

But Jesus does not label people as we do. He read the Pharisee's thoughts immediately. But instead of rebuking the pride-filled Jewish leader, Jesus told a story of a banker and two of his clients. One owed a large sum: five hundred denarii, well over a year's salary. The other man owed a small amount: fifty denarii, almost two months' salary. But the two men had fallen on hard times. They had no means to repay their debts. So the banker showed compassion and forgave both debts, large and small.

Jesus then asked a question: "Which one of them will love [the banker] more?" Simon the Pharisee did not hesitate: "I suppose the one who had the bigger debt canceled" (Luke 7:42-43).

Jesus nodded. Then he fired a direct accusation at the Pharisee. Traditional hospitality in those days included washing the guests' feet whenever they visited your home. Walking dusty roads with sandals left the feet dirty and tired. Washing your guests' feet said to them, "I am here to meet your needs. You are my special guest today—and for as long as you remain here." In this case, the woman's actions demonstrated humility.

But Simon had not humbled himself before Jesus. His lack of hospitality revealed the true nature of his character. The sinful woman, however, was authentic to the core. She did what Simon neglected—and at great cost.

Jesus knew the woman had a debt to pay. But not even the costliest perfume could pay for her sin—or anyone else's. Jesus, the compassionate Banker, forgave the woman's debt. Her humble act was suddenly transformed into a symbolic deed of love and gratitude. And Jesus used it to prove a point to Simon: "Her many sins have been forgiven—for she loved much. But he who has been forgiven little loves little" (Luke 7:47).

> Jesus does not label people as we do.

In between the lines, Jesus seemed to be saying to Simon, "You don't get it, do you? If you truly love God, as you Pharisees say you do, you would truly love others. If you understood what it means to be forgiven, you would not, could not, stop demonstrating that love. But you don't even know your heart is filled with darkness. It is boiling with prejudice, pride, and insincerity. This woman understands what you may never embrace—unless you have a heart change."

> God is not stingy with the blessing of forgiveness.

Jesus, brimming with compassion, turned to the woman and officially declared to her, "Your sins are forgiven." Then he commended her faith and said, "Go in peace" (Luke 7:48, 50).

Suddenly, the churning volcano stopped. The woman beamed with the light of Jesus' love and forgiveness.

God is not stingy with the blessing of forgiveness. All he asks is your authenticity and your admission of need—an exchange of selfish pride, of "I can do it my way," for "Lord, you are everything I need. I owe a debt I cannot pay." No begging, no pleading—just an agreement with God, like the drug addict's confession: "I cannot do it myself."

They are the words for which Jesus has been waiting. With tenderness yet bold authority, he smiles and reaches out to embrace you. Then he holds up his hand and writes *Canceled* across your debt. His death is the expensive perfume that washes away all the dirt of our sin-filled hearts. His love is the key that makes us whole again. And then to each he says, "Go in peace."

Everyone who receives his merciful blessing is changed. The darkness is gone. And the light never felt so good.

PERSONAL TRUTH

Because of Jesus, the only debt God's children owe is the debt of gratitude.

PERSONAL PRAYER

Lord, had you not paid my debt in full, I would be bankrupt by now. Thank you that your love reached down far enough to forgive me.

PERSONAL QUESTION

Do you have any debts that need canceling?

PRAISE AWAY YOUR ENEMIES

As [the nation of Judah] began to sing and praise,
the LORD set ambushes against the men of Ammon and Moab
and Mount Seir who were invading Judah,
and they were defeated.

—2 Chronicles 20:22

Most of us, when surrounded by an enemy, do one of three things: run, cry "Help!" or fight. But the king of Judah, Jehoshaphat, chose another battle plan.

When kings from three nations stood ready to attack his nation, Jehoshaphat appointed a men's choir to head up Judah's army. His men never planned to fire a single round of ammunition. No hurled spears. No hand-to-hand combat. The men's orders? I can hear it now: "On your mark, aim, *praise!*" Actually, Levites held an old-fashioned praise rally the day before the big battle. First King Jehoshaphat bowed down and worshiped, then the people followed suit. Next the Levites and other groups stood and shouted their praises.

The next morning, Jehoshaphat instructed his choir members to "praise [God] for the splendor of his holiness," saying, "Give thanks to the LORD, / for his love endures forever" (2 Chron. 20:21).

Can you imagine the delight of their enemies when they heard the choir warming up? I can just hear their whoops and taunts:

"Easy kill! Take 'em!" "Are they stupid or what? This one is a cinch!"

But that would be like a cocky running back slowing his dash to a trot because he thinks no one else is even close—he assumes his touchdown run is in the bag. He sees the opponent too late, as he is tackled within inches of his goal.

> Jehoshaphat's decision to praise God was not an afterthought or a shallow bargaining tool.

So it was with Jehoshaphat's enemies. An unseen force was fighting the battle for Jehoshaphat, and the king of Judah was only following God's orders: "Do not be afraid or discouraged because of this vast army. For the battle is not yours, but God's" (2 Chron. 20:15).

Did it work? Absolutely. As soon as the choir began to praise the Lord, God set up ambushes against Judah's enemies. Mass confusion erupted, and the enemy nations began killing one another.

You may be thinking, *Wow! All I need to do is start praising God, and my problems will disappear!* Maybe. Maybe not. Before you start celebrating your score this side of the goal line, you need to hear the rest of the story.

Jehoshaphat's decision to praise God was not an afterthought or a shallow bargaining tool. He was a man who knew God personally and knew how to appropriate God's blessings. The Bible says he experienced God's power and presence because he chose to walk with God in his early years (2 Chron. 17:3). As king, he completely devoted his heart to God and his ways (17:6). He always sought the counsel of God, even when others didn't (18:4). And when in peril, Jehoshaphat cried out to God for help (18:31).

Not only that, the king of Judah knew the wisdom of godly counsel. He gathered the prophets to get their advice on decisions—he wanted them to be based on God's laws, not man's

(2 Chron. 18:5). And when threatened, he asked the Lord for an answer, calling his people to pray and fast together. In every way, Jehoshaphat modeled publicly a life of praise and trust (20:3–12).

Chuck Swindoll once shared a story from his ministerial experiences overseas. He worked with a "maverick sort of a missionary" who, according to his wife, was dealing with great pressure in his life. The missionary spent much of his time ministering to thousands of soldiers on the island of Okinawa at the time. Swindoll went to visit him one night but was told he was probably at the office—located in a downtown area in a little alley. He got on a bus that rainy night and decided he would find Bob. He expected to find the missionary despondent and discouraged, considering the stress he was facing. But Swindoll found a different scenario.

As he approached the alley and the little hut office, he heard the singing of a familiar hymn. Swindoll stood quietly and listened to the sweet strains of that private praise service. Peeking through the walls of the cheap hut, he saw a man kneeling, hands raised toward heaven praising God. His Bible lay on one side and a worn hymnal on the other. It was obvious this was more than just an occasional event.

Again and again, the missionary read a Scripture passage, then sang a hymn to God. Swindoll said, "The remarkable thing is that the pressure that he was under did not leave for perhaps another two weeks, it seems. But that praise service alone before God absolutely revolutionized his life."[49] It's not the affirmative, praise-filled words that bring God's blessing, but the praise-filled life that honors him in every way. This kind of life sets God's power and presence in motion. Praise puts God on our side!

> It's not the affirmative, praise-filled words that bring God's blessing, but the praise-filled life that honors him in every way.

And not only does it bless God, it draws us to the very throne room where we are allowed to know him even better (Ps. 100:4). We don't bless the Lord to receive blessing but to know him even more deeply and completely.

And the more we know him, the more we want to live for him.

PERSONAL TRUTH

The answer to your problem may be just a praise away.

PERSONAL PRAYER

Lord, may everything I am and everything I do be an act of praise to you. You are an amazing God, and you are worthy of worship and praise.

PERSONAL QUESTION

Have you entered God's courts with praise lately?

KEEP ON ASKING

So Peter was kept in prison,
but the church was earnestly praying to God for him.

—Acts 12:5

They spent all night praying for his release from prison. Persecution had begun. And one of their own—one of Jesus' close disciples, James—had already been executed by the sword of Herod's anger. No doubt, Peter was next in line.

But the strength of God and the prayers of his people are more powerful than the plans of man. The night before trial, while Peter lay sleeping—chained between two guards—and the church continued praying, God sent his angel and touched Peter on the side to wake him. Peter was dazed, but after seeing the chains fall from his wrists to the floor, he followed the angel out of the prison past two guard stations until they arrived at the huge city gate. The gate creaked open, and the angel accompanied Peter to the end of the street, then left him alone.

But God never leaves us completely alone. Peter came to his senses and acknowledged immediately that he had witnessed the awesome power of God—and that his life had been spared. Peter had attended the School of Jesus for three years. He knew the power of prayer, and that the keys to the kingdom were wrapped up in that heavenly activity. When the disciples said, "Peter, we will be praying for you," he knew they meant it. Perhaps that's why

Peter headed to Mary's house where he knew the disciples were gathered to pray.

Thank goodness God sometimes chooses to answer even faithless prayers, for when Peter knocked on Mary's door and the servant Rhoda recognized his voice, she was so surprised that she ran back to the prayer meeting without even opening the door. "You're crazy!" they replied. But Peter's insistent knocking convinced them to open the door and see for themselves. Obviously they still had much to learn about the blessing of answered prayer (Acts 12:1–17).

> The strength of God and the prayers of his people are more powerful than the plans of man.

So did I. A couple of years ago I went on a mission trip to Peru with two dozen others from my church. We had prayed for months and asked God to do a great work, to make us useable, and for God to receive great glory from the trip. People prayed for us before and during our mission.

I was looking forward to sharing my faith and God's good news one-on-one, even door-to-door, if God so directed. We also wanted to encourage our fellow brothers and sisters in Christ throughout the churches we were visiting. When I discovered part of our task would be conducting vacation Bible schools, my stomach turned to jelly. I had taught in numerous Bible schools for many years, but that had been some time ago. I had primarily worked with adults for the last two decades. That was my comfort zone. Suddenly I began making excuses.

I struggled for weeks, then finally submitted as I prayed, "God, I'll do whatever you want, wherever you want. But you'll have to do it. Will you help me?" We were responsible for only one hour: teach a simple Bible story, color a picture, maybe sing a few songs. How hard was that? After all, translators would interpret.

The night before our VBS began, I discovered our teaching responsibilities would involve not one hour, but two. I slept only about three hours that night.

The next morning started off badly. We arrived at our assigned church thirty minutes late. I loved the children, but I struggled with filling the time slot, and felt a failure in my efforts to "teach." I assigned as much as I could to the musically talented teens accompanying our group.

That night three things happened that inevitably helped me to focus on God's part and less on mine. A minor earthquake shook our church building; the war with Iraq began, and I fell, ending up in a hospital emergency room with a golf-ball sized knot on my foot. During the wait, I found myself crying. Suddenly I didn't want to miss VBS the next morning! I actually *wanted* to be there. The only explanation I had for my change of attitude was that God had used these circumstances to get my attention. And at that moment I realized the importance of the message I wanted to share with the children the next morning. With this new development, God would surely have to intervene to make it possible.

My husband prayed for me publicly, and others did privately. The x-rays showed no broken bones, so I hobbled back to my room later with only a gauze ankle wrap. I was too tired even to worry. That night I slept like a baby. The next morning the swelling was gone, but then I was plagued with a Peruvian stomach problem. Once again, I said, "God, help! I cannot do this. Will you, please?"

> Thank goodness God sometimes chooses to answer even faithless prayers.

With a dry mouth I spoke to the children, then turned it over to the pastor with whom I had made arrangements earlier. I had shared in a simple object lesson how the children could come to know God personally through his Son, Jesus. I explained that

Jesus died for them because he loved them, and he wanted to help them live purposeful lives.

I sat down, bowed my head, and propped my foot up on a nearby chair. My stomach churned, and my arms felt weak, yet heavy—as if they were chained to the very chair in which I was sitting.

In a moment, I heard the pastor's voice, then some shuffling, and I looked up. Three rows of children had moved to the front pews. I looked at an interpreter quizzically. "The pastor asked all the children who wanted to receive Christ to move to the front pews," he whispered.

Tears began streaming down my face as I realized that seventeen children said yes to Jesus. *Only God could do that,* I thought gratefully. When the group returned to the states, we reported the results of answered prayer: about 170 people had come to know God personally that week.

I could identify with the man who went to Jesus and cried, "I do believe; help me overcome my unbelief!" (Mark 9:24). People prayed. And God answered—in spite of my own weak faith.

God taught me something else that week, and from Peter's experience. While the people prayed, Peter slept peacefully in prison. Both actions required dependence on God. Though the results may have surprised them, they recognized the hand of God, and God continued to use Peter.

Perhaps the real blessing of answered prayer is not getting the answer we want from God but in realizing our dependence on him, and in discovering more of what God wants from us. Ultimately, Oswald Chambers says, "the reason for asking is so you may get to know God better."[50]

In that case, I think I'll keep on asking.

PERSONAL TRUTH
Prayer changes the pray-er.

PERSONAL PRAYER

Lord, I want to get to know you better. May I never stop depending on you. Change my prayer—and my heart—that it might reflect yours.

PERSONAL QUESTION

What has God taught you about himself through prayer?

A Place to Belong

Praise be to the LORD,
who this day has not left you
without a kinsman-redeemer.

—Ruth 4:14

Perhaps you've attended a reunion where you encountered some not-so-pleasant family members. Bald heads, fat paunches, sour faces, and slow gaits had replaced the slim torsos, blonde curls, muscular frames, and sweet smiles you remembered from the last time you got together. But after all, ten—well, maybe twenty—years had passed.

Or maybe you endured off-color jokes, boisterous laughter, sleepless nights, and obtrusive personalities—and you were left wondering, *Where did all these people come from?* Maybe you heard about Aunt Bess's latest escapades in the nursing home, your cousin's drug bust, the preacher's latest bloopers, and your uncle's brother's wife's secret affair and unwanted pregnancy. It happens even in the best of families.

These descriptions don't by any means characterize every family get-together. Some reunions leave you laughing, encouraged, and more in love with your family than ever before. But maybe for you, right now, the idea of family being a blessing is far from your mind. And you're thanking God you're in your own home again.

That could be true even with some biblical families. But for the most part family meant everything to them—especially a place to belong. Hard times hit the family of Elimelech. A famine forced him and his wife and two sons to leave Bethlehem and go live in the country of Moab—a long way from their beloved Judea. Not long after, more tragedy struck. Elimelech died, leaving his wife, Naomi, and her two sons to live without him. The boys married, but ten years later, death stole their lives also. Three women, now widows.

> Sometimes God uses unbelievers, or the contagious joy of young believers, to show older ones the way back to his love.

When the famine ended, Naomi decided to return to her homeland. Why stay in a foreign land with no attachments—none except her two daughters-in-law? She couldn't ask them to leave their homeland, so Naomi urged Ruth and Orpah to stay. In strong relationships, someone always takes the initiative. Orpah reluctantly agreed, but Ruth begged Naomi to take her: "Where you go I will go, and where you stay I will stay. Your people will be my people and your God my God" (Ruth 1:16). Ruth had made up her mind. She was determined to go with her mother-in-law to a land of foreigners.

Was Naomi thinking of herself or of Ruth when in the prime of her grief she announced a name change that better fit her circumstances? "Don't call me Naomi," she whined to her friends when they arrived back in Bethlehem. "Call me Mara, because the Almighty has made my life very bitter. I went away full, but the LORD has brought me back empty" (Ruth 1:20-21).

The townspeople of Bethlehem didn't recognize Naomi at first. Perhaps the years had wrinkled her skin and turned her hair silver. Maybe she had added a few pounds or lost weight in her grief. Or perhaps the light had gone out of Naomi's eyes and face. A frown had replaced her familiar smile. The joyful woman who once filled their homes with laughter was now bitter, and maybe a little angry at God.

It is not God who makes us bitter. We choose our own responses when difficult circumstances enter our lives. Ruth, a Moabite, the despised enemy of Israel (Deut. 23:3), showed no sign of anger or resentment.

Sometimes God uses unbelievers, or the contagious joy of young believers, to show older ones the way back to his love. Once again Ruth took the initiative. The two women had no income, no means of support. But Old Testament laws—God's plan for such a time as this—provided for the poor. *Gleaners* were those who walked behind the harvesters to pick up leftover grain, intermittently scattered for them to harvest. This gave the poor an opportunity to "work" for their food—as farmers opened their fields to them at harvest time (Lev. 19:9–10). Ruth volunteered to go glean for their supper.

Obviously God had his hand in this atypical mother/daughter-in-law duo. Ruth gleaned in the very field of her mother-in-law's relative, Boaz. And he wasn't one of those not-so-pleasant family members. Boaz was kind-hearted—and wealthy. Besides that, he took the initiative to express a special interest in Ruth, providing all the grain she needed, drink when she was thirsty, and protection from wandering male eyes. Why would he do such a thing for a foreigner?

> Could it be that through the love and initiative of Ruth, Naomi found her joy again?

Word of Ruth's initiative and kindness spread fast in the small town. When Boaz heard what she had done, not only did he bless her, he even invited her to dinner. And Boaz made sure Ruth's gleaning sacks bulged with extra grain.

Naomi got so excited about her closest relative, Boaz, helping Ruth, that she decided to use her own initiative and play Cupid. Perhaps Ruth's newfound faith had rubbed off on Naomi. Her mother-in-law's thoughts of Ruth and her future seemed to overshadow her own claim to marriage and property.[51] (Of course, she could also have had grandchildren on her mind.)

Naomi carefully formed a plan, explaining to Ruth the Jewish principle of kinsman-redeemer: a close relative took care of needy persons in the extended family, sometimes by buying a piece of land the widow was selling. He thereby "inherited" the widow. So Ruth let Boaz know of her desire and need for a kinsman-redeemer. Another closer relative had first choice, but when he declined, Boaz bought not only Naomi's property, but that of her two sons. Boaz became their kinsman-redeemer and married Ruth, a much younger woman.

When did Naomi's bitterness end? How did she heal from grief? Nowhere else in the book of Ruth do we find anyone calling Naomi *Mara*. Could it be that through the love and initiative of Ruth, Naomi found her joy again?

To each character in this story, God gave the blessing of initiative—the active pursuit of kindness and love for another's good. That blessing multiplied. God kept on blessing with the gift of family, children, grandchildren, and even planting Ruth and Boaz in the direct lineage of Jesus Christ—who became the Kinsman-Redeemer of the world, the one who redeems us and gives us a place to belong.

All of these people enjoyed the blessing of family because of God's goodness, and perhaps because each person decided to think of another's needs as more important than his or her own.

PERSONAL TRUTH

Family is something all God's children can join.

Personal Prayer

Father, thank you for sending my Kinsman-Redeemer to give me a place in your family tree. As long as live, I will never forget the kindness and love you've shown me as one of your own.

Personal Question

Have you become a part of the family of God?

FAD-I-TUDE OR ATTITUDE

But seek first his kingdom and his righteousness,
and all these things will be given to you as well.

—Matthew 6:33

Living in simplicity is . . . well, a simple thing, according to some authors, and relatively painless as well. After all, it's just a matter of voluntary downscaling.

But if you were to ask one man about how painless it was to downscale, you would hear a different story. Jesus told a parable about a rich man who, when presented with the dilemma of a bumper crop so large it wouldn't even fit into his storage barn, couldn't bear to part with his abundance. The man decided the painless thing to do would be to bring in a local destruction crew to knock down the old barn, then hire a contractor to build a new, bigger one. Then he wouldn't have to worry about the future. He could take it easy, let the land lie idle, and enjoy the good life for many years. His definition of—or desire for—simplicity did not include denying himself anything (Luke 12:16–19).

Perhaps the one who thinks the path to simplicity is an easy journey has never tried to grow a garden or clean out a hall closet. Weeds choke our perspective, and the ordinary stuff of life so clutters our hearts, we sometimes don't know where to begin to find order again. And because simplicity is so hard to define, many of us never start the search. Yet if we are honest, our spirits long for this elusive blessing.

Is simplicity just about downsizing? Reducing our workload? Rearranging our time? Surrendering our surplus? Finding new retreats? Is it a trend that comes and goes with each generation? I once thought so.

> **Simplicity is not a "fad-i-tude," but an attitude.**

But Jesus' response to the rich man who built bigger barns indicates that simplicity is not so much a change in our physical situations as it is a change of our heart's desires. In the parable God told the man that he would die that very night, receiving only what he had prepared for himself. In other words, his treasures earned him nothing but false hopes and a tragic ending. Jesus ended his parable with these penetrating words: "This is how it will be with anyone who stores up things for himself but is not rich toward God" (Luke 12:21).

Simplicity is not a "fad-i-tude," but an attitude. The rich man never considered any other options for his bumper crop. His total reference for decision-making was himself, and his own well-being: "This is what *I* will do." And we are held responsible for the location of our desires. For wherever our hearts are, what we treasure the most will be there too (Matt. 6:21).

But simplicity is also a divine concept. Richard Foster says, "Simplicity is a grace because it is given to us by God. There is no way that we can build up our willpower . . . and attain it. It is a gift to be graciously received."[52] But who can receive it?

God tried to teach the Israelites something about this blessing when he provided unusual meals for them every day in the Sinai desert. Mysterious manna, a sweet substance that tasted like honey, fell daily from the sky like gentle snowflakes. God also gave some simple instructions for gathering the manna: glean only what you need for each day. But there are always some who reason, *What if? What if no manna falls tomorrow? I must store up extra today just in case. Maybe I should ration it, so I can experience this wonderful blessing when it stops. After all, nothing is forever.* But those who did so found their stored-up manna had bred worms (Exod. 16:14–20).

I truly believe that all of us desire to know this blessing of simplicity, but the real reason we shrink back from it is fear. Even greed stems from fear. The greedy, rich fool who built bigger barns, and the children of Israel who ignored God's instructions, feared the future and tried to control it by hoarding. Is it any different for those of us who stockpile hours of work to appease the fear of a jobless future? Those of us who fill our lives with ceaseless activity may do so out of fear that we will miss something important.

Or we may fear the guilt and disapproval of saying no, when in reality, we may be choosing something *good* at the expense of God's *best.* On the other hand, saying yes may be too difficult because, out of fear, we allow ourselves no discretionary time for options.

When surgeons opened up former President Bill Clinton's chest in a follow-up heart surgery, they found scar tissue around his heart in the form of a hard plaque substance that lined half of his lung. It had to be peeled away like an orange for him to resume his full breathing capacity.

It's easy to allow the scar tissue of fear to line our hearts and close off our ability to breathe in truth. We can suggest many disciplines— many surgeries—that might help us downscale and remove what can become the physical hindrances to simplicity. But these are only an outward expression of an inner desire, and they don't always stem from pure motives. And is *less* a one-size-fits-all lifestyle? If we are not "rich toward God," as Jesus said

> If we are not "rich toward God," as Jesus said of the rich fool, downscaling does no good.

of the rich fool, downscaling does no good. Unless we allow God to peel away the layers of fear, one by one, we will be back in the hospital repeatedly.

Jesus says there is a better way. In fact, it's so simple we may miss it. He says to first address the real problem: "Look at the birds. Observe the lilies. They don't worry about food, store up goods, or stress out working too hard. Your heavenly Father provides their needs. Will he not also take care of you, who are much more valuable to him than the nature he created for you?"

And then Jesus added the clincher. "Seek first his kingdom and his righteousness, and all these things will be given to you as well" (Matt. 6:33). Foster says, "There are not many things we have to keep in mind—in fact, only one: to be attentive to the voice of the true Shepherd. There are not many decisions we have to make—in fact, only one: to seek first his Kingdom and his righteousness. There are not many tasks we have to do—in fact, only one: to obey him in all things."[53]

Jesus says he has provided enough of everything we need. Practicing an attitude of simplicity—living trust-filled, fear-free lives—is a matter of the heart. Downscale your fears; upscale your faith. When your heart seeks to make Jesus the center, that's where your real treasure will be. That's when you truly become "rich toward God."

The heart—and blessing—of simplicity is ordering our lives so we can see, hear, and obey God at every turn.

Personal Truth

We do not find simplicity by discovering who we are; we find it by discovering who God is.

Personal Prayer

Jesus, may everything in my life so revolve around you that every thought, every decision, and every action reflects you. Teach me when to say yes and when to say no. Teach me to live simply, trusting you each day for every provision.

PERSONAL QUESTION

What fears have you been hoarding lately?

GOD'S FOOTPRINTS

In the beginning
God created the heavens and the earth.

—Genesis 1:1

The first time I stood at the lookout point near Lake City, Colorado, I gasped. It was a misty morning, the air crisp and cool and fresh—alive with magnificent wonder. Who would think a name like Slumgullion Pass could contain such beauty? Yet as I looked at the massive snow-covered peaks, circled by angelic rings of clouds, tears began to bathe my cheeks. The majestic footprints of God were all over the place.

We love Colorado. Every time I cross the state line, something wells up inside me begging for expression. It is by far one of our favorite family vacation states ever since I first witnessed its beauty as a small child.

But my world has expanded in that time, and I've witnessed endless wonders in God's creations. To think that in the beginning the world was one vast, dark space—until the Lord stepped in and opened his mouth, saying, "Let there be light! Let there be Day! Night! Sky! Land! Seas! Plants! Trees! Sun, moon, stars!" And with each part of creation, the suspense escalated. "Birds! Fish! Animals!" Until the crowning glory when God made man and woman in his own image (Gen. 1:1–27).

God reveals so much of himself to us in nature, and we can see his tracks everywhere we go.

John Glenn, the first American astronaut to orbit the earth, saw some of God's footprints in his first space adventure. Glenn says he mentally collected beautiful sunrises and sunsets as "an art collector remembers visits to a gallery full of Picassos, Michelangelos, or Rembrandts." Yet he said even that wonderful man-made art could not compare to God's masterpieces in the reds, oranges, and yellows of the sun's beauty. He couldn't wait to see those sunsets and sunrises through "heavenly" eyes. Here is how Glenn described that experience in space:

> **God reveals so much of himself to us in nature.**

It was even more spectacular than I imagined, and different in that the sunlight coming through the prism of Earth's atmosphere seemed to break out the whole spectrum, not just the colors at the red end but the greens, blues, indigos, and violets at the other. It made spectacular an understatement for the few seconds' view. From my orbiting front porch, the setting sun that would have lingered during a long earthly twilight sank eighteen times as fast. The sun was fully round and as white as a brilliant arc light, and then it swiftly disappeared and seemed to melt into a long thin line of rainbow-brilliant radiance along the curve of the horizon. . . . I added my first sunset from space to my collection.[54]

Even the intricate design of each creature God made can only point to an omniscient, omnipotent, yet tender Creator. For example, the woodcock can sense vibrating motion underground with its feet. This bird knows instinctively to spread its wings and begin flapping them rapidly against the ground. Why? Because the earthworms below know that in a drenching rain they will

drown if they do not crawl to the surface quickly. When the woodcock mimics rain by flapping its wings on the earth's surface, the
worms rush to the top. The woodcock hears their movement and
injects its bill, catching them on their way up the earthy elevator.[55]

In the otter, we see a fun-loving God; in the eagle, we respect his
majesty, protection, and gentleness. The lion reminds us of his
power; the sparrow, his careful provision. The Bible mentions four
small wonders that are "the wisest of the wise":

> Ants—*frail as they are,*
>> *get plenty of food in for the winter;*
> marmots—*vulnerable as they are,*
>> *manage to arrange for rock-solid homes;*
> locusts—*leaderless insects,*
>> *yet they strip the field like an army regiment;*
> lizards—*easy enough to catch,*
>> *but they sneak past vigilant palace guards.*
> (*Proverbs 30:24–28* MSG)

But perhaps nothing can compare to God's intricate work as
seen in the formation of a baby and its birth.
What mother hasn't been awestruck the first
time she saw at only a few weeks the tiny out-
line—fist, profile, and head, the complete tiny
curved body of her own flesh-and-blood baby,
no bigger than her thumbprint—recorded on
the doctor's sonogram? What mother's heart
hasn't skipped a beat the first time she heard

> God *wants* you to see his world, his works, and himself through heaven's eyes.

the gentle *ka-thump, ka-thump* of her own baby's miniature heartbeat in the early weeks of pregnancy?

And yet not everyone recognizes the blessing of God's beautiful
handiwork. Why is that? Perhaps it is because, as Tozer says, "We

have lost the ability to wonder." We can't see God with our naked eyes and live, but we can experience his blessing of creation—the blessing of wonder. We "can hear Him sing His song of creation and redemption. And we can feel the pressure of His breath upon us as we move through the world."[56]

Those who will shed their preconceived knowledge, their frantic paces, and their crowded spaces will begin to see the Creator's footprints everywhere they look. These delicious treats are not forbidden fruit, like the tree in the first Garden of Eden. God *wants* you to see his world, his works, and himself through heaven's eyes.

With him, the wonders never cease.

PERSONAL TRUTH

It is difficult, if not impossible, to love the Creator and hate his creation.

PERSONAL PRAYER

God, what a wonder you are! You are the Author and Creator of everything beautiful—and to think that I get to enjoy it. Help me to value these blessings—the things and the people you made—as much as you do.

PERSONAL QUESTION

Have you made any mental collections of God's handiwork lately?

FREE AT LAST

It is for freedom that Christ has set us free.
Stand firm, then, and do not let yourselves
be burdened again by a yoke of slavery.

—Galatians 5:1

Abraham Lincoln's Emancipation Proclamation contained powerful words. It was a powerful act. It spelled freedom! Yet many emancipted men, women, and children continued to live like slaves—as though Lincoln's declaration of truth were a lie. Who would choose slavery again, even though they are free? And why?

Onesimus did. He couldn't believe it when he first heard Paul's "emancipation proclamation." Onesimus remembered his days of slavery. No one could forget that. Even though his master, Philemon, had been a kind man, Onesimus had wanted to be the master of his own fate. So one day he gathered up his meager belongings—and maybe even some of his master's—and set out on his own. But everywhere Onesimus showed his face, he carried with him an invisible label: runaway slave. And only the one in bondage knows that until he is proclaimed free, he will always remain a slave.

But then Onesimus met Paul, and everything changed. He heard Paul talk about the time he was a slave himself—a slave to his own desires. The apostle Paul also knew what it was like to be denied freedom from his stays in prison, yet he had also discovered another secret: he had encountered Jesus in a dramatic way (Acts 9). And no doubt he spoke some of Jesus' words to Onesimus, words the disciples probably passed on to Paul during his ministry: "Then you will know the truth, and the truth will set you free" (John 8:32).

> Only the one in bondage knows that until he is proclaimed free, he will always remain a slave.

The runaway slave embraced the truth of that proclamation, and he was a Christ-one, truly a free man. He and Paul evidently agreed, however, that it was time for Onesimus to return to Philemon. But why? Why would a free man enter slavery again? Did he not understand the meaning of freedom?

Paul himself spoke to the people in Galatia, encouraging them to stand firm in their freedom—not to be "burdened again by slavery." Although the two—the Galatian Jews and the Gentile slave Onesimus—were now free, they both understood the shackles of slavery. The Galatian Jews once believed lies and were slaves to the Law and their own interpretations of it. They could not accept Jesus by faith as the fulfillment of that Law. But they, too, had discovered the truth of who Jesus really was. For them to go back as slaves to powerless laws would nullify Jesus' death and resurrection.

It was a different story with Onesimus. Selfishly, Paul could continue to use Onesimus's help, but he knew a Christian's debts must be paid, not ignored. When Onesimus stepped back into Philemon's household, he would be embracing a voluntary slave position—and that made all the difference.

By Roman law, Philemon could prosecute and call for Onesimus's immediate execution. But Paul considered Onesimus a son, and in a letter to Philemon, Paul pleaded with him to welcome his former slave with forgiveness in the same way he would welcome Paul.

He even dared to offer a reason for their separation in the first place: so that Onesimus's relationship with Philemon would no longer be as slave, but now as a brother (Philem. 16). And in between the lines Paul seemed to say, "Because in Christ we are all one and are all brothers."

It sounds as if Paul was talking more about the blessing of slavery than of freedom. It all depends on how you look at it—and how you define it. The Bible says a man becomes a slave to whatever masters him (2 Pet. 2:19). If after hearing the truth of Christ's "emancipation proclamation" we turn back to harmful lifestyles and destructive behaviors, that kind of slavery is not a blessing. When we allow things such as fear, worry, bad habits, or anger to control us, we can become slaves to those old masters.

A woman named Sera struggled to know the difference between freedom and slavery. She cleaned houses for a living, and her clients bragged about her spotless work. But Sera had a weakness: she loved beautiful things.

Windows were not the only things that sparkled in her customers' wealthy homes. One woman kept her jewel boxes in plain sight, unlocked, filled with diamond bracelets and other gemstone rings. Like a curious child, Sera couldn't resist trying on a few of the exquisite pieces. But eventually that curiosity turned Sera into a thief. Her client didn't even miss the jewelry.

> If Jesus, who is the Truth, is truly our Master, then we are in bondage to him and him alone.

Sera hid the jewels until a crisis in her life forced her to sell them at a pawnshop. She moved away with no forwarding address. But Sera never forgot her foolish act. Everywhere she went, she felt as if people were staring at a big *T* for *Thief* branded on her forehead.

Three years later, Sera's life changed when a Christian neighbor told her about Jesus. Sera embraced her newfound faith and knew at once what she must do: she drove to a nearby police station and turned herself in. The only problem was, no one had filed a report. The police called the woman from whom Sera had stolen, and Sera told her the story, asking her forgiveness. She was ready to serve her punishment. But the woman chose not to press charges.

But Sera had a new Master. Sera enlisted a jeweler's help to estimate the approximate value of the gems she remembered stealing. For the next ten years, she worked hard to pay back the money for the jewels. Every paycheck, she sent a small amount to the wealthy woman. The day finally came when Sera's debt was paid in full. Sera was no longer a slave to her past.

Is it possible to be a slave and yet remain free? Sera and Onesimus would say yes. If Jesus, who is the Truth, is truly our Master, then we are in bondage to him and him alone. What a paradox that the one to whom we devote ourselves has already declared us free. Yet only by choosing to become his slaves can we experience that freedom (Rom. 6:22). Only then can we access the power and desire to love the one we serve—and to love others around us. No matter how people may choose to label us, if we know Christ, we are free indeed.

That is what makes both slavery—and freedom—a blessing.

PERSONAL TRUTH

What you don't know can hurt you.

PERSONAL PRAYER

Lord, when lies threaten to pull me away from you, remind me of the truth: you are my Master and Lord. I choose to be enslaved by your love. Thank you for paying for my freedom.

PERSONAL QUESTION

To whom or what are you enslaved?

THE MEASURE OF TRUE BEAUTY

When this is done, I will go to the king,
even though it is against the law.
And if I perish, I perish.

—Esther 4:16

When a young Jewish woman first arrived at the Medo-Persian Beauty Contest and saw a huge harem of beautiful women, I wonder if she thought, *What* am *I doing here?* Perhaps she observed their flawless complexions, beautiful clothes, and graceful statures and thought, *I'm so plain. My skin is imperfect. Maybe I'm too short. Is my hair too dark?* No doubt she asked a hundred other questions fueled by doubt and insecurity.

But Esther needn't have worried. Her beauty would prove powerful enough to fulfill a dangerous quest: saving the lives of her people.

Before Esther arrived at the Persian palace, King Xerxes, drunk and loose-tongued, foolishly ordered his wife, Vashti, to parade before a room of gawking men—apparently without her traditional veil.[57] When she refused to lower herself, the king not only dumped his queen, he made a decree for all women to give ultimate respect to their husbands (Esther 1:10–21).

Historians say this same impulsive king once ordered the son of one of his loyal subjects cut in two, when the father tried to excuse him from the military draft. And *this* was the man who might choose Esther for his queen?[58]

Along with all the other women in the "contest," Esther submitted to a year's worth of beauty treatments. What woman wouldn't look beautiful after that? Then one day, she looked in her "mirror" and heard the king say, "I choose you" (Esther 2:9, 17).

Most of us tend to judge beauty as we do a book: by the cover.

Most of us tend to judge beauty as we do a book: by the cover. God says, "Man looks at the outward appearance" (1 Sam. 16:7). Robert Browning noted, "It is not our job to remake ourselves, but to make the best of what we have." Obviously Esther had made the most of the external portion of her beauty. So Esther became a queen.

But someone else had been watching Esther long before she entered the palace. And though she took care to make the outer self beautiful, it was just that: an exterior. God's beautification program had started years before in the heart of this young Jewish girl. Although we are not told much about Esther's beliefs, we do know that God chose to use her. William MacDonald says, "God is the Author of all history, even if He does not sign His name at the bottom of every page."[59] When God looked in Esther's heart, he saw a woman of inner strength and beauty, one who could act like a queen in a crisis, unafraid of danger and loyal to her people even if it meant death.

Was God wrong? Not hardly. Behind all the events recorded in the book of Esther, we see God's hand orchestrating every event, and God's signature at the bottom of every page. Esther's cousin, Mordecai, uncovered a sinister plot by a wicked, greedy man named Haman. Jealous of Mordecai, who refused to bow to and honor him, Haman tricked the king into signing an irreversible decree to annihilate all the Jewish people.

Mordecai revealed the plan to Esther and told her she faced a choice: "Don't think for a moment that you alone will escape this decree just because you live in the palace. If you aren't willing, someone else will be raised up for this task. Perhaps you were born for such a time as this, Esther!" (see Esther 4:13-14).

Heavy assignment—especially when it could mean Esther's life. The king had not called for her in thirty days, and to approach the king without his summons meant instant death—unless the king held out his royal scepter to her. At that moment, perhaps Esther heard a divine voice speak to her heart: "The most beautiful of all is the one who is willing to obey my call. Will you be that one, Esther?"

Instead of seeking counsel from her maids, she asked them, along with all her Jewish people, to fast for three days. On the third day, Esther boldly approached the king—and faced death. But the king extended his scepter, and Esther's courageous act and humble requests persuaded Xerxes to spare the Jews.

Esther's last recorded act in the Bible stamped *True Beauty* on her legacy for all time. Together with Mordecai, who then sat second in command to the king, she authorized the celebration of Purim—a feast that is still honored today—in remembrance of a sacred moment in history when God preserved his people (Esther 9).

> In the end, true beauty is not defined by a flawless complexion, a tiny waistline, or ample curves.

Some believe beauty can be a curse or a blessing, depending on what one does with it. But in the end, true beauty is not defined by a flawless complexion, a tiny waistline, or ample curves. It is not limited by race, status, or even gender. God's evaluation is always accurate. When others saw a simple shepherd boy in David, God saw a king (see 1 Sam. 16:1-13). When others saw only a young Jewish girl, God saw a queen. The Bible says that God does not focus on our physical characteristics but measures beauty by a different Book: he looks at the cover of the heart. And when God sees a flawless heart, a small ego, ample courage, and a surrendered life that reflects his own—God says, "That's true beauty."

And that's the kind of life God chooses to bless even more.

Personal Truth

Beautiful hearts never go out of style.

Personal Prayer

Lord, thank you for seeing true beauty in all of us. Keep us looking at your mirror, not our own. Help us to reflect your beauty in everything we do.

Personal Question

Whose mirror are you holding?

RIVAL OR SERVANT?

He must become greater; I must become less.

—John 3:30

Few men or women enter the world knowing exactly why they were born. Yet John the Baptist understood. How did he know? Did his parents spell it out for him as a young boy? Each time he spoke of his own dreams, did they snatch those visions and replace them with a Calvinist decree: "What will be must be"? Did they drill him unmercifully, "You must always play second fiddle to your cousin. He will always be better than you"? Did his choice to live in the desert as a wild and wooly preacher evolve as a result of crushed hopes and cruel comparisons?

Hardly. The Bible says that as early as several months before his birth, even while nestled in his mother's womb, John the Baptist leaped with joy at the presence of his cousin's growing embryo in Mary (Luke 1:41, 44). An unborn baby expressing emotion—and communicating to its mother, aunt, and another unborn child: how could this be?

The Bible says through the words of Gabriel, the angel of God, that even from birth, John the Baptist would be filled with the Holy Spirit (Luke 1:15). Incredible! Jesus, consummated by the Holy Spirit himself, and his cousin, both filled with the Spirit since birth—both born with unquestionable destinies.

The very first time John recognized Jesus even in the womb

says something about his servant nature. John's mission was to "go on before the Lord, in the spirit and power of Elijah." Why? "To turn the hearts of the fathers to their children and the disobedient to the wisdom of the righteous—to make ready a people prepared for the Lord" (Luke 1:17). From the beginning, John was to be a carpet for Jesus' feet and a banner advertising the Messiah's coming.

> What plan God maps out for us may not be nearly as important as in what spirit we accomplish it.

Would parents knowingly direct their son to second-place servanthood when everything inside them longs to see their child excel in first place? Probably not—unless God makes perfectly clear that child's role—and theirs—from the very beginning. And from the time of John the Baptist's birth unto his death, we are never given any indication of a struggle to dishonor God's purpose or to divert his plans for selfish reasons, by either parent or John the Baptist himself. Even though Zechariah, John the Baptist's father, had a difficult time believing he and his wife could bear a child in their old age, he understood clearly that child's unique purpose (Luke 1:5–80).

Most of us long to know and struggle to discern our exact purpose in this life. What will we be? What are we to do? How are we to serve? And although we may never be chosen for such a lofty purpose as John the Baptist, the forerunner of Christ, we each have an assignment, a purpose that fits into God's grand scheme for eternity. And the Bible says God will fulfill his purpose for us (Ps. 138:8).

Part of that purpose is to bring honor to God: to know him, serve him, delight in him, and make his ways known. How do we do that? What plan God maps out for us may not be nearly as important as in what spirit we accomplish it. God wants to develop our character. He wants to make us more like him. What are our ultimate motives? Whom are we trying to please? Do we hope to gain something—or do we long to give something away?

Mark it down: testing will come. It did for John the Baptist. Even in his unconventional dress and wild mannerisms, he was popular—and scores of followers called him the "Baptizer" (see Mark 1:4-8). Yet no one could accuse him of trying to score points in popularity contests. Calling his audience "You brood of vipers" was not exactly the way to win friends and influence people (Luke 3:7).

John the Baptist soon encountered a rival, someone just arriving on the scene. Was he a threat to John's success? No, just his cousin. Were they competitors as kids? Did they see each other often? Did they speak of their futures and anticipate such a time as this? We don't really know. But we do know that when the Holy Spirit fills and equips a person for a task, he is the one doing the work. He is the one controlling the desires, giving direction and conviction, and he is the one motivating with purpose.

John the Baptist did not snatch his own opportunity to prove he was great, not even when some people were wondering if John was the promised Messiah (Luke 3:15-16). Some even tried to pull John into an argument and reported that Jesus was attracting more followers than John (John 3:25-34). Instead, John remained steadfast in accomplishing what he was born to do: he chose to become less, so others could recognize and acknowledge Jesus as the greater. Both Jesus and John were born for servanthood. But only one was the Son of God. Both were baptizing. But only one "baptize[d] . . . with the Holy Spirit and with fire" (Luke 3:16).

> When we intentionally make Jesus greater, we experience an even bigger blessing than we thought possible.

John's heart did not swell with power but was humbled by love. He understood the wonderful blessing of humility, from birth until his violent death by beheading (Matt. 14:3–12). Unafraid of the truth, John was driven by a Spirit greater than his own to accomplish his purpose in life.

He became less so Jesus could become greater. And God exalted him (Matt. 11:7–14). Jesus himself said to two of his disciples, both vying for greatness in God's kingdom, "Whoever wants to become great among you must be your servant, and whoever wants to be first must be your slave—just as the Son of Man did not come to be served, but to serve, and to give his life as a ransom for many" (Matt. 20:26–28).

Where can we learn servanthood? From the Chief Servant of all: God's own Son. And when we do, the blessing of humility God gives us lifts us higher than the position we might have coveted in pride. Living to make others, rather than ourselves, successful does not come naturally. But when we intentionally make Jesus greater, we experience an even bigger blessing than we thought possible. Pastor/college professor John Mason said, "The casting down of our spirits in true humility is but like throwing a ball to the ground, which makes it rebound the higher toward heaven."

The blessing of true humility is one only God can give—and those who are blessed with it are usually unaware of it.

Personal Truth

Rivals rarely arrive at the same conclusion.

Personal Prayer

Lord, I, too, must always become less so that you will be seen as the greatest one in my life. For as long as I live, may I honor you with my whole heart.

Personal Question

Who is the star in your life?

UNFAILING LOVE

Sow for yourselves righteousness;
reap the fruit of unfailing love,
and break up your unplowed ground;
for it is time to seek the LORD,
until he comes and showers righteousness on you.

—Hosea 10:12

The pain of another's unfaithfulness is like a knife slicing through the heart. Some might extend grace once. But what would you do if your spouse repeatedly engaged in extramarital sex—with no intention of changing? Most would file for divorce after the first offense.

But not Hosea. How could a prophet of God preach about holiness and purity when he couldn't even influence his own wife? And why did he continue to torture himself, rescuing his wife from another man's arms and raising children that were not even his own? What drove a man to endure such pain?

God often uses unusual methods in relating to his people, and at times he instructed the prophets to do what we might consider bizarre. But his purpose in doing so was always to demonstrate a godly characteristic of himself and a visual lesson for his people. When the northern nation of Israel continued to deteriorate in its rebellion, God called a simple sheepherder named Hosea as his personal spokesman to get the people's attention.

At the heart of God's activity, you will always find a deep, intimate love. And he wanted to use Hosea to show Israel how its "prostitution" with other gods was breaking God's heart. Time after time, like soap-opera sirens, the Israelites chased after the gods of their heathen neighbors instead of honoring God as their one true Husband.

> At the heart of God's activity, you will always find a deep, intimate love.

So God asked Hosea to take a woman who would act out the very lifestyle that his people had chosen; Hosea married a prostitute. He loved her deeply, even when she broke his heart repeatedly. He loved even those children other men had fathered.

Then one day Hosea faced a final humiliation. His wife, Gomer, ended up on an auction block in the public square, haggard and hopeless. We can only imagine the jeers that people threw at Hosea: "Is this your 'wife,' Hosea—if that's what you want to call her? Whose wife is she really?"

And then the bidding opened. "Who will bid for this . . . this worn-out piece of humanity?" No one seemed interested in used property. Finally, a lonely, bearded man walked from the back of the crowd. His shoulders were stooped, his eyes filled with pain, but his lips parted with a slight smile. "Fifteen shekels of silver and ten bushels of barley!" boomed the voice of the prophet.

A gasp rose from the crowd. Fifteen shekels for this ragged excuse for a woman? Ten bushels of barley just to endure another broken heart? No one else bothered to challenge. The bidding stopped. "Sold!"

Hosea obeyed God and brought Gomer back home—again to illustrate God's great love for unfaithful Israel (Hosea 3:1).

This time the prophet whisked his wife away on a private retreat, not allowing her to continue her intimate connections with any man. Love demanded some drastic intervention without being harsh, demanding, or cruel. Hosea would "live with her"—or a clearer meaning would be *wait* for her to return his love (Hosea 3:3)[60] The children's names, which first represented God's anger and judgment on Israel, would change, demonstrating God's desire to reverse curses to blessings (Hosea 1:6–11, 2:23).

God wanted to shut the nation of Israel up to himself, away from idols and influences that would prostitute their hearts. Why? Because of his unfailing love. So that his people would wake up and return to him (Hosea 3:5).

Ray Johnson's mother, Martha, believes in unfailing love. Doctors diagnosed the former Dallas Mavericks basketball player with a rare, fast-moving form of cancer called acute promyelocytic leukemia. By the time Martha arrived at the hospital in Alabama, Ray was in a coma. Ray was shut up in intensive care for the next seventy days. Martha stayed with him. She wallpapered the place with 270 e-mails, hung streamers, kept records, wrote in her journal, prayed, and warned scores of visitors—to stay positive. Above all, Ray's mother believed.

At one point Ray's body bloated, his toes turned blue, and his normal weight of 176 had swelled to 236 pounds. Former Mavericks assistant coach Donnie Nelson said Ray looked like a corpse. Then the miraculous happened: "One day, out of one prayer or a thousand, Ray's eyes fluttered." He woke up. No brain damage. Just a long recuperation—but a treatable illness. The doctors called it a miracle. His weight dropped to 128 pounds. The lack of oxygen to his body created something like frostbite, and he lost all the toes on his left foot and two on his right. But there's one thing he didn't lose: the unfailing love of his mother and friends.[61]

> When we were hopeless and haggard on the auction block of the public square, God bought us back with the price of his own dear Son.

"No pain, no gain" is rarely a welcome truth—in marriage, in families, in friendships, or even in theory. Broken hearts want instant mending. Broken lives want instant healing. And as a result, many never experience the blessing of unfailing love, simply because they throw in the towel too quickly.

That's when it's good to remember our roots. Sshh! The bidding has begun. A hush settles over the crowd, but then murmurs fill the room. "Will no one bid?" pleads the auctioneer. Out of the back someone walks slowly to the front. The person on the auction block appears lifeless. The bidder extends his palms, showing the scars of his love. And from his smiling lips booms a loving voice: "I have already paid the price: my life for this one."

Perhaps you are that worn-out piece of humanity. Weary, broken, disillusioned, ashamed—the circumstances don't matter. With the tenderness of a loving mother or father, God picks you up and carries you to his "intensive care," where he wants to nurse you back to health. He will wait as long as it takes, in the hopes that you will wake up—and experience for yourself the life he wants to give you.

God never stops loving. He paid the ultimate price for us even though we "all . . . have gone astray" (Isa. 53:6). When we were hopeless and haggard on the auction block of the public square, God bought us back with the price of his own dear Son.

Then, as God did for Israel when he "led them with cords of human kindness, / with ties of love" (Hosea 11:4), he shut us up to himself so he could show us his great love and tenderness.

The result—the blessing—that comes when God's love flows through us, is a supernatural devotion far beyond our natural abilities. That blessing is the sweetness of being shut up in God's intimate presence and a love relationship with him that will never die.

PERSONAL TRUTH

God never gives up, never gives out, never gives less than his best for you. He never stops waiting—for you to wake up and come home.

PERSONAL PRAYER

Lord, I will never understand your unfailing love and the tenderness with which you shut me up to yourself. Thank you for rescuing me from the auction block of my shame. Help me never to give up on others.

PERSONAL QUESTION

How has God's unfailing love affected you?

GIVING TO GET?

"I tell you the truth," he said,
"this poor widow has put in more than all the others.
All these people gave their gifts out of their wealth;
but she out of her poverty put in all she had to live on."

—Luke 21:3–4

Anyone can give, but not everyone is generous. That's what Jesus seemed to be saying when he presented a powerful truth to his disciples.

An alms box, placed in the outer court of the temple, gave people an opportunity to give their money to the poor. Young and old, rich and destitute, knew this was their religious duty. After all, for the poorest huddled just outside the temple, on public corners, on the steps throughout town, or near the city gate, others' gifts were their prime means of livelihood.[62] The temple offerings, if handled rightly, helped to provide basic sustenance for the blind, the lame, the weak, the unfortunate.

In observing people, Jesus didn't miss a thing. Through his heavenly eyes, he viewed more than the money dropped into the box or the people who put it there. Jesus looked at the motives of every giver. And as he watched the rich deposit their offerings, he also noted a poor widow. Jesus saw through the multiple bank accounts and checkbook balances. He knew the rich gave out of fat pocketbooks, and that was notable, although many gave for show as well. A wealthy man might place a one-hundred-dollar bill in the plate, a drop in the bucket from his weekly stash. But this poor widow passed by and slipped two small copper coins in the plate. Compared to the rich man's gift, financially her offering was close to nothing.

Jesus inferred that you can't afford *not* to give.

Jesus said many gave out of their abundance, but the woman gave from her poverty. She gave all she had. Perhaps she understood Jesus' words: "Give away your life; you'll find life given back, but not merely given back—given back with bonus and blessing. Giving, not getting, is the way. Generosity begets generosity" (Luke 6:38 MSG).

The widow obviously didn't agree with the excuses some might offer: "I cannot afford to give." Jesus inferred that you can't afford *not* to give. It is God's plan of economy, his way of meeting needs.

Am I saying you should give to every good cause, regardless, just so you can receive more money? No. Others have milked unsuspecting donors out of millions of dollars, suggesting the Bible guarantees them returning wealth. If the poor widow had given with that motive, Jesus' story would have been different. Nowhere does he indicate that her motives were distorted.

But giving and then receiving in return *is* a biblical principle. Perhaps Paul amplified this truth well: "Remember: A stingy planter gets a stingy crop; a lavish planter gets a lavish crop" (2 Cor. 9:6 MSG). God is looking for cheerful givers. What happens when such a person is generous with what he has received from God? The Bible says God will give him more than enough "so that in all things at all times, having all you need, you will abound in every good work" (2 Cor. 9:8).

Put those verses together and let's say it even more simply: when you give generously to the Lord for legitimate needs that honor him, he will give more back to you. So you can buy more stuff? No. So you can give more generously to the needs God shows you, so he can give more back to you, so you can keep giving to him to minister to people's needs. Paul added, "This most generous God who gives seed to the farmer that becomes bread for your meals is more than extravagant with you. He gives you something you can then give away, which grows into full-formed lives, robust in God, wealthy in every way, so that you can be generous in every way, producing with us great praise to God" (2 Cor. 9:10–11 MSG).

This principle applies not just to financial blessings but to any way that God has blessed us. Blessings are to be shared, not hoarded. Oswald Chambers says, "We are to be fountains through which Jesus can flow as 'rivers of living water' in blessing to everyone. . . . As surely as we receive blessings from Him, He will pour out blessings through us. But whenever the blessings are not being poured out in the same measure they are received, there is a defect in our relationship with Him."[63]

Whether we have little or much to offer does not matter to God. He can take the widow's mite, like the lunch of a little boy, and feed thousands if he so chooses (see John 6:5–13). God wants our gifts to come unreserved from the heart. When that happens, God promises more blessings than we can hold.

One family understood well the term *channel of blessing*. Mother Teresa said a man came to her house one night to tell her about a family with eight children who needed food. Mother Teresa took some rice to the mother. The mother promptly divided the rice into two portions and hurried out with half of it. When she returned, Mother Teresa asked the woman where she had gone. Her simple answer: "To my neighbors—they are hungry also!" Mother Teresa said, "I was not sur-

> "Remember: A stingy planter gets a stingy crop; a lavish planter gets a lavish crop."

prised that she gave, because poor people are really very generous. But I was surprised that she knew they were hungry. As a rule, when we are suffering, we are so focused on ourselves we have no time for others."[64]

Those who are truly generous see the needs of others. They understand that the Giver of every good and perfect gift allows us to share in the blessing of generosity. They know it is not a burden but a joy to be treasured—*and* shared.

PERSONAL TRUTH

Those who give unselfishly will always have numerous blessings to count.

PERSONAL PRAYER

Lord, thank you for the privilege of giving—and receiving. Forgive me when I selfishly hoard your blessings rather than lavishing them on others. May I always be a channel of your blessing to others.

PERSONAL QUESTION

What has God given you to share?

Our Real Home

I am going . . . to prepare a place for you.
And if I go and prepare a place for you,
I will come back and take you to be with me
that you also may be where I am.

—John 14:2–3

All of us grow weary at times of battling temptation, wrestling with habits, coping with pain, facing death. Some have no earthly idea what heaven is like, but they do want it to be an end to negative experiences. Just what *is* heaven like, anyway?

In his book *Heaven,* Dr. Randy Alcorn says, "Many people find no joy at all when they think about Heaven." A pastor once told him such thoughts made him depressed. His idea of heaven? Floating around on clouds, strumming a harp: b-o-r-i-n-g.[65]

But heaven—or the "New Earth," as Alcorn refers to it—is so much more than the end of something negative. And it will hardly be boring (Ps. 16:11). It is both the beginning and a continuation of something grand and glorious, something beautiful and indescribable—something that is beyond our imaginations.

In her book *Heaven: Your Real Home,* Joni Eareckson Tada explains something of that "much more" of heaven. She says a photographer uses a negative image to show us a positive image. As an artist Joni uses the same principle; for example, first painting the sky around a leaf without outlining the leaf first—allowing the sky to define the shape of that leaf. In this way, "the artist helps you see by painting what you don't see."[66]

Joni says it's the same principle when we think about heaven. Negatives help show us the positive. On earth, the negatives are suffering, misery, and death. The positive side is the opposite. Revelation 21 talks about some negatives in heaven as well: no more sorrow, no more crying, no more pain, and no more curse.

> **Heaven is so much more than the end of something negative. And it will hardly be boring.**

Even imagining the positive side of heaven, few writers or artists have done heaven justice. Their most exquisite descriptions are at best a shadowy image of the real thing.

Alcorn, a leading authority on heaven, goes a step further and agrees it's true the Bible says, "No eye has seen, / no ear has heard, / no mind has conceived / what God has prepared for those who love him." But he points out the rest of the biblical sentence: "But God has revealed it to us by his Spirit" (1 Cor. 2:9–10).[67]

That's precisely what God did for the apostle John. God gave a snapshot of heaven to the only one of Jesus' twelve disciples who escaped a violent death. Banished to the island of Patmos, the beloved John recorded in the book of Revelation for us what God revealed to him in the Spirit. Here we see the most descriptive picture of heaven, our final home, that God has ever given to us: a "new Jerusalem, coming down out of heaven from God, prepared as a bride beautifully dressed for her husband" (Rev. 21:2).

As John was carried away in the Spirit to a "mountain great and high," he saw that city made of pure gold and described it in great detail as brilliant with jewels, shining with the glory of God and the Lamb.

John continued to write of heaven as a real *place* of substance where a river flows by trees with real fruit—the end of decay, impurity, and sin—a description that sounds very much like Eden.

Alcorn says we all long for that perfect world of Paradise that Adam and Eve first experienced in the Garden of Eden. He adds, "And that is exactly what God promises us—a home that will not be destroyed, a kingdom that will not fade, a city with unshakable foundations, an incorruptible inheritance." He reminds us we came in after the Fall, so we never saw the original earth as God first created it. "God will not scrap his original creation and start over," says Alcorn. "Instead, he will take his fallen, corrupted children and restore, refresh, and renew us to our original design."[68] God is even now at work daily in his children, renewing and reshaping us in his image. Both Randy and Joni agree that in our final home, we will, for the first time, become the persons we were always created to be.

When recording Revelation, I'm sure John remembered well Jesus' words to the disciples at their last supper—about the home he was preparing for them (John 14:2). Alcorn says that *home* is not just a metaphor. It is

> *a place promised and built by our bridegroom; a place we'll share with loved ones; a place of fond familiarity and comfort and refuge; a place of marvelous smells and tastes, fine food, and great conversation; a place of contemplation and interaction and expressing the gifts and passions that God has given us. It'll be a place of unprecedented freedom and adventure.*[69]

If those words are accurate, I look forward to boundless energy (the complete healing of fibromyalgia), never again breaking God's heart through sin, telling a story without forgetting key details, and writing books with greater understanding (and perhaps rewriting past ones I penned with such limited knowledge).

If we have a choice, I'd like to memorize "Clair de Lune" on the piano, even learn new instruments, write a new praise song with which to worship Jesus, grow perfect roses, and ask lots of questions. I want to talk to all the saints, thank all the people who touched my life, meet the child I lost in miscarriage, see all my family members, search for the people I prayed for over many years, and a hundred other joyful activities.

> In our final home, we will, for the first time, become the persons we were always created to be.

The blessings of heaven God designed for us include too many things to mention. The most beautiful garden, the most intimate and satisfying love encounter between a man and a wife, even the sweetest moments of fellowship on earth with our Lord are but a millionth of a fragment of the incredible joys we will experience in heaven. We will inhale the fragrance of God and cry with longing, "More! More! More!" And God will satisfy.

But the best blessing of all is finally seeing the one for whom we have longed, the one we have served and loved, the one who designed us for this eternal place called home—and then returning that love and praise, living with him forever.

To the one who has said yes to Jesus, heaven means going home—to him. It's a blessing reserved for those who know him personally—and it's the blessing I treasure most.

PERSONAL TRUTH

Home is where God waits with open arms and says, "Welcome, my child. Welcome!"

PERSONAL PRAYER

Lord, I may not understand all that you have waiting for me in heaven, but I long for it—and you—with every fiber of my being. Thank you for every disappointment, every loss, every challenge on earth. Help me to see those things through new eyes and share with all those I know how much you want them, too, to find a home in your eternal family.

PERSONAL QUESTION

When was the last time you really longed for heaven?

AUTHOR'S NOTE

Perhaps you have never come to know and enjoy the intimate presence of God personally. If he has placed such a desire in your heart, may I share with you some simple steps so you can become acquainted with him and become a child of God forever?

1. Admit the sin in your life and the need in your heart for God (see Rom. 3:23).

2. Acknowledge that Jesus loves you and that he died for your sin (see John 3:16).

3. Recognize his salvation is a gift, not something earned (see Eph. 2:8–9, Rom. 6:23).

4. Ask Jesus to forgive you, to come into your life, and to fill you with his personal, intimate presence (see Rev. 3:20).

5. By faith, thank him that you are now God's child, and confess that from now on, he will be the Lord and Love of your life. Give Jesus the keys to all the rooms of your heart (see Rom. 10:9–10; John 1:12).

I hope this book has encouraged you. If I can help your Christian growth in any way, please let me know. You can drop me a line at my Web site: www.rebeccabarlowjordan.com.

—Rebecca Barlow Jordan

NOTES

1. William MacDonald, *Believer's Bible Commentary* (Nashville, Tenn.: Thomas Nelson Publishers, 1995), 48.

2. Max Lucado, *In the Grip of Grace* (Dallas, Texas: Word Publishing, 1996), 38, 40.

3. Ibid., 123.

4. Jill Lieber, "Donating Hair Supply Is Kids' Sweet Dreams," *USA Today Sports,* December 14, 2004, http://www.usatoday.com/sports/2004-12-14-hair-donation_x.htm (accessed January 31, 2005).

5. Donald Bradley, "A Parent's Goodbye," *Kansas City Star,* reprinted in *Dallas Morning News,* June 25, 2000, 7A.

6. Janice Elsheimer, *The Creative Call* (Colorado Springs, Colo.: Shaw Books, 2001), 51–52.

7. Elsheimer, *Creative Call,* 20, 80, 89.

8. Philip Yancey, ed., *The Student Bible* (NIV), (Grand Rapids, Mich.: Zondervan, 1986), 435.

9. John Foxe, *Foxe's Book of Martyrs,* ed. W. Grinton Berry (Grand Rapids, Mich.: Fleming H. Revell, 1998), 12–13.

10. Paul Montacute, "Hunger in Southern Africa: Our People Are Forced to Eat Roots and Leaves," in a news release from Baptist World Alliance, November 15, 2002, http://jmm.aaa.net.au/articles/10410.htm (accessed February 12, 2005).

11. James Forbes, pastor of Riverside Church in New York City, "Hunger in a World of Plenty" (no date given), http://www.churchworldservice.org/pdf_files/Faces/Hunger/pdf (accessed February 16, 2005).

12. The Associated Press, "Little Progress in Hunger Fight," from CBSNEWS.com, December 8, 2004, http://www.cbsnews.com/stories/2004/09/21/world/main644763.shtml (accessed February 16, 2005).

13. A. W. Tozer, *Tozer on the Almighty God,* comp. Ron Eggert (Camp Hill, Pa.: Christian Publications, Inc., 2004), January 3.

14. Ted Engstrom and Robert Larson, *Motivation to Last a Lifetime* (Grand Rapids, Mich.: Zondervan, 1984).

15. Shirley Montee, *May's Boy: An Incredible Story of Love* (Nashville, Tenn.: Thomas Nelson, Inc., 1981).

16. William Barclay, "The Letter to the Hebrews," *The Daily Study Bible* (Edinburgh, Scotland: St. Andrew Press, 1955), 137–138.

17. Rick Warren, *The Purpose-Driven Life* (Grand Rapids, Mich.: Zondervan, 2002), 17.

18. *Webster's New World Dictionary*, Second College Edition (New York: Simon & Schuster, Inc., 1986), 20.

19. John Eldredge, *Wild at Heart* (Nashville, Tenn.: Thomas Nelson Publishers, 2001), 5, 13–14.

20. Ibid., 16, 15.

21. Ibid., 6.

22. Henry Blackaby and Claude V. King, *Experiencing God: Knowing and Doing the Will of God* (Nashville, Tenn.: The Sunday School Board of the Southern Baptist Convention, 1990), 19.

23. MacDonald, *Believer's Bible Commentary*, 1264.

24. Ibid.

25. *The Student Bible*, 1062.

26. Don Richardson as told by David Brickner, "Peace Child," *Jews for Jesus Newsletter*, December 1997, http://www.jfjonline.org/pub/news/letters/1997-12/peacechild.htm, (accessed February 22, 2005).

27. "Presidential Medal of Freedom Recipient Katherine Graham," http://www.medaloffreedom.com/KatherineGraham.htm (no date or writer given), (accessed April 12, 2005).

28. Laura Griffin, "The Fervor and the Solace," *Dallas Morning News*, August 29, 2004, 1E, 7E.

29. Henry Drummond, *The Greatest Thing in the World* (Great Britain: Collins, London and Glasgow, 1962), 50.

30. Eugenia Price, *God Speaks to Women Today* (Grand Rapids, Mich.: Zondervan, 1964), 172.

31. "Regional Honorees: Make a Difference Day Awards," *USA Weekend*, April 2001, http://www.usaweekend.com/diffday/honorees/2001/2001winnersm_z.html (accessed February 23, 2005).

32. Nanci Hellmich, "Where Charity is Always at Home," *USA Today*, December 24, 1997.

33. *Webster's*, 876.

34. Barbara Johnson, *Fresh Elastic for Stretched-Out Moms* (Ada, Mich.: Fleming H. Revell, 1986).

35. F. N. Peloubit, ed., *Peloubit's Bible Dictionary* (Philadelphia, Pa.: The John C. Winston Company, 1947), 360–361.

36. Blackaby and King, *Experiencing God*, 75.

37. Dietrich Bonhoeffer, *The Cost of Discipleship* (New York: Simon & Schuster Inc., Touchstone edition 1995), 89.

38. Ibid., 100.

39. Chris Tiegreen, *At His Feet* (Wheaton, Ill.: Tyndale Publishers, Inc., 2003), 83.

40. MacDonald, *Believer's Bible Commentary*, 1348.

41. Thomas à Kempis, *The Imitation of Christ* (Mt. Vernon, N.Y.: Peter Pauper Press, n.d.), 61.

42. *Webster's*, 732.

43. Al Bryant, *1,000 New Illustrations* (Grand Rapids, Mich.: Zondervan, 1964).

44. Tozer, *Tozer on the Almighty God*, February 23.

45. *Webster's*, 1421.

46. Kevin Miller, "Life's Game Plan," *Secrets of Success* newsletter (no date given), http://www.secretsofsuccess.com/people/gibbs.html (accessed March 7, 2005).

47. Ibid.

48. Ibid.

49. Swindoll, *Tardy Oxcart*, 627–628.

50. Oswald Chambers, *My Utmost for His Highest* (Grand Rapids, Mich.: Discovery House Publishers, 1992), March 20.

51. MacDonald, *Believer's Bible Commentary*, 291.

52. Richard Foster, *Freedom of Simplicity* (New York: HarperCollins Publishers, 1981), 7.

53. Ibid., 184.

54. John Glenn with Nick Taylor, *John Glenn: A Memoir* (New York: Bantam Books, 1999), 263.

55. Institute of Basic Youth Conflicts, Inc., Character Sketches, vol. 1 (Chicago, Ill.: Rand McNally and Company, 1976), 80–85.

56. Tozer, *Almighty God*, March 9.

57. MacDonald, *Believer's Bible Commentary*, 498.

58. *The Student Bible*, 453.

59. MacDonald, *Believer's Bible Commentary*, 496.

60. *The Student Bible*, 779.

61. Kevin Sherrington, "Ray of Hope," *Dallas Morning News*, January 21, 2005, 1C, 5C.

62. George M. Mackie, *Bible Manners and Customs* (Old Tappan, N.J.: Fleming H. Revell Co., n.d.), 144–45.

63. Chambers, *My Utmost*, September 7.

64. Mother Teresa, *No Greater Love* (Ignacio, Calif.: New World Library, 1997).

65. Randy Alcorn, *Heaven* (Wheaton, Ill.: Tyndale House Publishers, Inc., 2004), 6-7.

66. Joni Eareckson Tada, *Heaven: Your Real Home* (Nashville: Lifeway Press, 1996), 18-19.

67. Alcorn, *Heaven*, 18.

68. Ibid., 78, 112.

69. Ibid., 440-441.